New American Funerals

New American Funerals

Creating and Delivering Nonreligious End-of-Life Ceremonies

A Guide for Professional Celebrants

Elizabeth Nordberg Stokes
Humanist Funeral Celebrant

18th and Fairfax Press
Cambridge, MA

First softcover edition September 2022

Cover design by 18th and Fairfax
Cover photographs by Joshua Fuller

ISBN 979-8-9866961-0-2 (softcover)
ISBN 979-8-9866961-1-9 (ebook)

18th and Fairfax Press
Cambridge, Massachusetts

Acknowledgements

Because this book was started in 2020 during the Covid-19 pandemic, it owes much of its existence to the patience, goodwill, and humor of my two children, Ben and Will. Without their jump scares, snuggles, wrestling moves, puns, and an inordinate number of episodes of Star Trek, this book would undoubtedly be a lesser thing.

Thank you also to Kathy and Maura for tending our friendship throughout the pandemic. Though you might not have known it, you listened to many of the seedling ideas contained in this book. Our conversations, step counts, and persistent support of each other's endeavors has meant the world to me.

Donna Forsythe, director of *Celebrant Academy*, played a major role in the book's existence. Donna saw something in my celebrancy style (and hopefully substance!) that she thought was worth nurturing. My students at CA also helped shape the book into something practical and usable. The end-of-life space is typically very solitary, so their real-time company and feedback was treasured. The ongoing camaraderie of my fellow teachers at Celebrant Academy was also instrumental in my ability to see this book through.

A special thanks goes to Greg M. Epstein, with whom I had early conversations about Humanism, atheism, and agnosticism. His encouragement to take on the role of humanist funeral celebrant, as well as his leadership in a national conversation about humanism, were pivotal in helping me see myself as a representative of this philosophical outlook.

On the page, Jennifer Valero has been a reliable and easy editor to work with, and a welcome second set of eyes. However, all errors remain my own, especially since I have a difficult time calling any manuscript "finished.

The origin story for this book owes a great deal to one of my own teachers, Vince Vanston. In his creative writing and English classes, he created a welcoming space of genuine intellectual freedom and imagination. He was also a funeral director, and treated us students as complete and vital human beings just as we were. Coming from someone who saw death every day, this sentiment was visceral, rare, and invaluable. I'm grateful for his dark humor, freewheeling positivity, and effortless encouragement.

Last but not least, a special thanks to my parents, Kevin and Denise, for modeling the craft and theory of existentialism, life rituals, and ethical leadership.

The land I live and work on is the traditional land of the Neponset Band of the Indigenous Massachusett Tribe. Thank you to the elders, past and present, for their stewardship of this land through many generations. A portion of my income goes to the tribe, and to organizations run by and for Native, Black and LGBTQ+ people.

Learn about and support the Massachusett Tribe at Ponkapoag.

Support Black, BIPOC, and LGBTQ+ voices and rights with The Trevor Project, It Gets Better, Sage, Equal Justice Initiative, National Bailout, and NAACP Environmental & Climate Justice.

Support our living planet with Environmental Defense Fund, Natural Resources Defense Council, and 350.org.

Table of Contents

INTRODUCTION   I

PART 1.

AMERICAN DEATH, DYING, AND END-OF-LIFE CUSTOMS   1

Why Do We Ritualize Our Dead?   3

What Is an American Funeral?   9

Disposition Options   11

Who's Who in End-of-Life Services   17

Roles and Responsibilities of the End-of-Life Celebrant   21

The Variety of End-of-Life Ceremonies   25

PART 2.

FUNERAL DESIGN   35

Funeral Design   37

Typical Funeral Ceremony Elements   43

Main Written Parts of the Ceremony   53

Writing and Delivering Eulogies   61

Committal Services   71

PART 3.

PERSONALIZING END-OF-LIFE CEREMONIES   75

Place and Setting   77

Readings   79

Music   83

Rituals   87

Difficult Ceremonies   95

PART 4.

DOING THE WORK   107

Funeral Celebrant's Workflow   109

Handling Inquiries   115

Handling Family Interviews   121

Conducting the End-of-Life Ceremony   127

PART 5.

THE BUSINESS OFEND-OF-LIFE CELEBRANCY   **131**

Business Models   133

Connecting with Community   141

The Future of Funerals   145

PART 6.

APPENDIX   **151**

Glossary of Terms   153

Sample Inquiry/Intake Form   161

Sample Service Agreement   163

Sample Interview Form   167

Sample Ceremony Outline   173

Sample Committal Outline   177

Online End-of-Life Services   179

Sample Funeral for a Public Figure   183

Public Speaking Practice   185

Notes   189

Bibliography   199

Author Biography   215

Introduction

If you are a professional celebrant working in the United States, welcome! It may feel as if there are very few of us, since the role is still new here. But we are here and, along with other nonreligious end-of-life service providers such as death doulas and a new generation of funeral directors, we are poised to support a growing number of people who want meaningful, nonreligious funerals.

Partly due to technology (both its capabilities and constraints), partly due to the Covid-19 pandemic, and undoubtedly due to changing beliefs and behaviors, people are now more than ever seeking a deeply satisfying coda to their life and the lives of those they love. As the majority of the population moves away from organized religion[1] toward other expressions of community, connection, and a life lived in harmony with one's values, the need for nonreligious ceremony has also increased. Striving to honor a life with a ceremony that emphasizes human endeavors such as love, discovery, creativity, and interdependency is a core task for us as individuals and as a species. Death is one of the few things that still happens to everyone, and that happens only once, at least for now!

When I started teaching at Celebrant Academy, I struggled to find a book that covered everything I thought an end-of-life celebrant would want to know to do this work confidently. So, I ended up writing and piecing together different lessons of my own. Those lessons turned into this book, the book I wish I had when I was learning. It aims to provide a solid foundation for how to create nonreligious end-of-life ceremonies that reflect our current humanist worldview. You won't find lists of sample ceremonies and rituals. Off-the-shelf material won't cut it in a culture that still seeks—against a backdrop of megacorporations and algorithm'd content—genuine recognition and customization for this essential life event.

You will find modular elements you can arrange to craft personal end-of-life ceremonies, ways to easily conceive custom rituals for funerals, and refreshing strategies for writing eulogies. I also share end-of-life knowledge usually shielded behind privacy and tradition, and the work behind the scenes you rarely see: How exactly do you let the grounds crew know when to lower the casket? What if the grandchildren are too distressed to do the ritual you practiced? What do you need to consider for an ash scattering?

I also wanted to offer straight talk on areas of contemporary American celebrancy such as the industry racial and gender imbalances, business models, and the economic context in which American celebrants work. Finally, I have attempted to acknowledge some of the cultural changes in America today that we humanists welcome. The book recognizes a variety of pronouns, sets out to make clear social biases around end-of-life services, and brings attention to voices and cultures that have been historically marginalized.

You can see that the words *new* and *American* in the title of the book are no accident. It's my hope that this book extends and updates the good work that has come before it. Han Hills's *The Humanist and Non-Religious Celebrant Handbook* (2015) and Corliss Lamont's *A Humanist Funeral Service and Celebration* (2011) in particular informed and guided me when I was starting out as a celebrant. They are two of the few books written for the American celebrant, and of even fewer that cover funerals. Celebrants are more common in other English-speaking countries such as Scotland, England, and Australia (where the role was first established in 1973),[2] but funeral logistics, customs, and traditions are very different in those countries from ours here in the United States.

The word *professional* is also intentional. There are many books for families who want to set a ceremony in motion when someone dies, and even more for people under deadline to write a eulogy. This book is for the professional funeral celebrant who needs to know how to do this work for a living and at an emotional distance from the families they serve.

Throughout the book you'll find the words funerals and end-of-life used almost interchangeably.

End-of-life is becoming more accurate because it covers a broader range of services. Perhaps a better phrase will evolve, however, because end-of-life is unwieldy to read and often results in typos! Feel free to forge your own term if it better describes your offerings and outlook.

The material in this book is supported heavily in the Celebrant Academy class with knowledge, experience, creativity, and up-to-date resources shared with and among other new and seasoned celebrant students. They also bring a cultural, generational, and regional variety to every interaction that enriches our work. If you are an experienced celebrant, however, you should be able to use this book on its own to start creating and delivering fledgling funerals.

Whether you are a new celebrant or one polishing your craft after many years, it is my hope that this book will offer you practical, contemporary, and inclusive tools for becoming the best end-of-life celebrant possible.

Part 1.
American Death, Dying, and End-of-Life Customs

Why Do We Ritualize Our Dead?

Based on the work of Dr. Alan Wolfelt.[3]

We can find examples of the importance of funerals across millennia and media, from Homer's *Iliad* when Achilles refuses to return Hector's body to his family, to Marvel's *Black Panther*, who reassesses his father upon learning that he let his own brother's death go unmarked. At its most essential, the funeral is a communal and choreographed set of steps for those closest to the deceased to take as they arrange the bodily remains. The correct treatment of a dead body is considered an essential element of membership in a community. While particular customs and etiquette vary from culture to culture, ignoring or violating those customs is almost uniformly taboo.

And yet, according to research and trends, in these early years of the twenty-first century people are not asking themselves what kind of funeral to have, but rather whether to have a funeral at all.[4] Add to that the inability to hold funerals during the height of the Covid-19 pandemic. Did this further erode the idea that we should mark deaths formally, or did it renew this feeling? We'll have to see.

In light of these trends and events, what purpose do funerals serve us? Why do we ritualize the bodies of our dead? Dr. Alan Wolfelt has studied grief, loss, and bereavement for decades. He articulated a hierarchy of needs that funeral customs satisfy:[5] *reality, recall, support, expression, meaning,* and *transcendence*. I've paraphrased these below.

Funerals help us confront a new reality

Funerals are a set of prescribed, administrative actions that help us acknowledge the fact that someone has died. They help carry us over this unfamiliar and unwanted threshold. We confront the impermanence of the physical bodies of those we are in close relationship with.

Funerals help us adjust from a future with the deceased, to a future of memories recalled about the deceased

Funerals begin the process of shifting our experience with the deceased from someone we can create new experiences with, to someone who exists only in our memory. We offset the loss of the physical, living body of the deceased by gathering memories. We survey the past in order to label it as "The Past" and to help us turn toward the future.

Funerals are an opportunity for support

By their very nature, funerals are communal ceremonies that provide distinct ways for friends, family, and acquaintances to show support. From sharing stories about the deceased that create a full picture of who they were, to providing food, or just by "filling the seats" to indicate that the deceased made a difference, was loved, and impacted people. When the primary mourners stand or sit in certain places, wear certain clothes, or have specific roles, they are recognized as the ones who are the focus of our support.

Funerals are a container in which we express feelings

Funerals are a socially accepted place for our large, unwieldy, and uncomfortable feelings about death, loss, and relationships. Funerals give us permission to grieve unlike almost any other setting. Funerals are also an expression of our love and connection to the deceased.

Funerals give meaning to both life and death

Funerals take the specifics of one person's life and show how those choices and relationships reflect universal human values. A funeral transforms the unique life of the deceased into something more persistent, such as a legacy. As mourners acknowledge the legacy of the deceased, they are reminded of their own impermanence and invited to grapple with how to make their own lives meaningful.

Funerals telegraph a new social status and invite us to transcend our former identity

When someone dies, our social status often changes in a way that communities recognize. Whether we become widowers, orphans, elders, or the last of our clan, we mark that this death changes our relationship to our community, and to our own identity. How, or whether, we accept this new identity is a task for the years following a loss.

You can learn more about the purpose of funerals by exploring Dr. Wolfelt's work. In my time as a funeral celebrant, I have also come to see three other essential purposes that funerals serve:

Funerals keep mourners present and embodied for this difficult task

If you have ever gone through a difficult separation, you know how easy it is to feel disconnected from your body. You might stop feeling joy in activities, or you stop eating or sleeping. Autopilot kicks in and days pass. It is not exactly depression, but rather numbness. Funerals are a way to help those who are grieving to stay present in their bodies. Whether it is through dressing in special clothes, watching a slideshow, singing, standing in attendance, or casting dirt atop the casket, these funeral rituals (action added to symbolism) invite the grief stricken to stay present and to remain among the living.

Funerals mark time

Ceremonies of all kinds ask us to step outside our normal activities and mark an event as so special it only happens once. Because of this, they become the relative punctuation of our lives. They provide mile markers for where we are in our own lives. You will hear people say, for instance, "Was that before or after Deshawn's funeral?" or "It was about two months before my sister died." Funerals, because they are often accompanied by sharp, sudden emotions, play this role strongly. Even years after a death, there will be an instinctive moment of silence when someone mentions a death as a reference point in time.

Funerals reinforce our status as human

Funerals are something that define us as human, so much so that for a long time it was thought that only humans ritualized their dead.[6] Humans who did not were considered barbaric, and people who do not afford the dead a "proper" burial in their own culture may still be considered dishonorable. In most places, mistreatment of a dead body is criminalized. Even for people with whom we had difficult relationships, we do them—and ourselves—a service by marking their death to maintain our own humanity. The ritual advertises that we are good citizens by adhering to the values and behaviors of the human community.

In talking about the purpose of funerals, it is also worth talking about what funerals are *not*. Funerals are not tools for imposing emotional states on mourners nor invalidating the emotional states they are in. That is, the funeral should not be used to make mourners happier or sadder than they are.

Many people reference Elisabeth Kubler-Ross's concept of the stages of grief,[7] and celebrants can get it in their minds that the funeral functions as a step forward in these stages of grief. Kubler-Ross's stages have been reviewed and critiqued over the years, but even when first published the stages of grief referred to the process that the dying go through, not mourners.[8] Yes, the funeral creates an emotional journey for attendees by using story and symbolism, but it must meet the primary mourners emotionally where they are.

As an example, it would be easy for a celebrant to presume that a very formal, somber end-of-life ceremony is the most appropriate approach for a still-born baby or someone who has ended their own life. A celebrant might be uncomfortable with families who do not seem *sad enough*, and decide to craft a ceremony so that mourners can "confront their grief." (Celebrants are not alone in this well intentioned maneuver, but professional funeral celebrants are held to different standards than friends and acquaintances of the grieving.)

The trouble with this approach is that grief can look different from moment to moment and day to day. It can be expressed through joy, happiness, and appreciation just as much as it can be expressed by sadness or despair. It is not necessarily something to move beyond or extinguish.[9]

The other problem is that deciding what mourners *should* be feeling obstructs rather than eases whatever emotional process the primary mourners are actually feeling. If the NoK says the ceremony for their child or relative should be an upbeat experience, you need to find ways to attain that skillfully and sensitively.

Bringing an open and non judgemental mind to family meetings will help families trust you, and will help you create end-of-life ceremonies that resonate with truthfulness, meaning, and creativity.

What Is an American Funeral?

Over time, pop culture has homogenized many death customs and practices in the United States. But the United States is a vast and diverse country. Cultures, rituals, and traditions around death still vary depending on where you are in the country, the history of the area, and whatever communities, affinity groups, and/or subcultures the deceased and their family feel a part of. You may encounter indigenous people; people displaced due to war, climate or economic need; people brought to the United States unwillingly; people who have immigrated by choice; and descendants of all of the above.

You'll meet people who bring a strong tradition to funeral practices and those who want to create new ones to mark their evolving experiences. An ease of movement within the borders of the United States, coupled with the swift decrease of Christianity[10] and rise of the nonreligious (or unaffiliated),[11] means that many people you encounter in the United States may not have any traditional or religious models in mind when it comes to arranging a funeral.

Within all of these groups, you will find groups that are forging new ways to express identity, acknowledgement, and validation through death. Notable groups in our country to educate yourself about and be open to include Native American, Black/African American, and LGBTQ cultures. But do not assume that end-of-life wants, needs, challenges, and practices are uniform within any group. Contemporary nonreligious funerals are above all a thoughtful blending of what is uniquely individual with what is universally human.

Some end-of-life customs that you may not see in mass media, but which are common in parts of the United States, include the second line parades of New Orleans,[12] RIP T-shirts[13] (southern Black culture, but now widespread), roadside memorials[14] (originating in the southwest as *descansos*) and ghost bikes,[15] funeral-fundraising car washes, the surfer's memorial circle (or paddle out),[16] and mortuary bands.[17] The variety is stunning and reflects a large and dynamic population, as well as traditions that have evolved and new ones that have been created.

Further, even among the nonreligious there may be religious practices that have solidified into cultural traditions. Beliefs and biases about social class, status, and wealth will also come into play even if they are not mentioned explicitly. The conditions are usually ripe for major social elements like these to rise to the surface. In general, people arrive at death—their own or a loved one's— wanting to feel, at this vulnerable moment, part of something larger than what they may have experienced in a long time.

In addition to ceremonial practices, the funeral logistics, design, and disposition methods are also influenced by environmental realities such as flood plains, seasons, and soil type. Six feet under is deeper than bodies actually need to be buried,[18] but it depends on local conditions and laws. The above-ground cemeteries in New Orleans, the tightly stacked cemeteries in urban areas, the recomposition options in the Pacific Northwest, and the winter church graveyards of New England are all shaped by the environment. Environment may mean climate, weather, terrain, or other natural elements that over time influence how a community handles its dead.

As a celebrant your job is to be respectful of the variety of traditions you will encounter wherever you are. Be open to bridging traditions, religions, or cultural rituals, and be familiar with the common requests and dispositions you will see in your area. This will allow you to create authentically American ceremonies, whatever that means for your communities and conditions.

Disposition Options

Disposition is a technical term for the disposal of a body. For most people, disposal is too unpleasant a term, so we call it the disposition. It is what we do with the physical remains of the body. It is the way in which the body is physically at rest, whether that is by being buried (in a casket, or shrouded, or with no protective or symbolic covering), being cremated and turned to ash, or being slipped into the ocean for a burial at sea. These are all examples of dispositions.

The most common dispositions in the United States right now are cremation and conventional (whole body) burial.[19] The term disposition gets a little blurry when you are talking about the specific method of how the body will be handled, versus the final ceremonial gesture to put the body at rest. For example, someone may be cremated, and then it might also be called the final disposition when their urn is placed into the ground or into a columbarium niche.

WHAT FAMILIES EXPERIENCE IMMEDIATELY AFTER A DEATH

As a celebrant, you usually will not know about events immediately surrounding the death, and it will not matter too much to your work, but it is helpful to know what families are going through before you first meet them.

In the case of a home death, families might choose to keep the body of the deceased at home. All states allow this as long as there is attention to temperature of the body.[20] A visiting doctor, hospice nurse, medical examiner, or coroner may pronounce the death and create a death certificate.

In nursing home and hospital deaths, the institution will have standard policies in place and existing partnerships with funeral homes and crematoriums. Often the deceased is removed from the room quickly so that another patient can move in; however, families are still legally allowed to bring their family members home after death. Communicable diseases and public health emergencies have some impact on this, but even those who die with disease are usually able to be brought home with some extra care. If families want a homecoming, they should make any needs known as soon as possible (ideally before death) so that things can proceed calmly after the death. Contacting a hospital chaplain can help with expressing these needs and having them recognized by the hospital.

In the case of traumatic death, with significant insult to the body, options for bringing a body home and specific dispositions may be limited.

Some bodies may be required to undergo an autopsy. Some bodies may have organs or tissue harvested (donated). It is almost always still possible for them to be presented for open casket viewing and such. In some cases (e.g., infectious disease) the body may be required to be cremated. Bodies usually cannot be legally cremated within forty-eight hours of death in case there is a need for an autopsy but it varies by state.[21]

DISPOSITION METHODS

Below are disposition methods, listed in alphabetical order. Following that are the environmental impacts and general costs of various dispositions. Refer to the Glossary in the Appendix for any unfamiliar terms.

Alkaline Hydrolysis ("Aquamation" "Chemical disposition")
- A mix of water and chemicals returns the body to its primary chemical components with an ash-like result
- Gray water from the process is sometimes used productively in agriculture
- Implants and devices are removed after the process, but before dealing with larger pieces of bone
- Many states currently allow for human disposition in this way: Alabama, California, Colorado, Florida, Georgia, Idaho, Illinois, Kansas, Maine, Maryland, Minnesota, Missouri,

Nevada, North Carolina, Oregon, Utah, Washington, and Wyoming. Others are considering laws allowing the process.

Burial (Conventional)
- May be a direct burial (no viewing, visitation, or other ceremony) or a burial with a ceremony
- The body is in a casket and is often embalmed
- The casket is interred in the ground, within a concrete liner, or immured above-ground in a tomb, crypt, or mausoleum

Burial (Green/Natural/Traditional)
- No embalming or interventions are used to preserve the body
- Any toxic or non-natural implants or devices are removed
- Shrouding or casketing is in only natural or biodegradable material
- Neither a metal liner nor a concrete liner surrounding the body are used
- Interment is in a conservation cemetery, hybrid cemetery, or on private land
- Note that many religious and cultural groups practice, and have practiced, green burial for some time. This term is entering the mainstream mostly because it flows against current Christian and Anglican practices, and because it connects with concerns about environmental sustainability.

Burial at Sea
- Whole body burial at sea can be in a biodegradable casket or shroud with weights, or an ash scattering
- Burial must be at least three miles from shore and requires special permitting

Cremation
- The body is burned, often along with a container (though not always the coffin the body was in for any viewing or ceremony). The body is reduced to bone, and bones are crushed to ashes.
- Direct cremation is when the body is taken from place of death to the crematorium without ceremony
- Witnessed cremation occurs before, after, or as part of a funeral ceremony. Family, friends, or a ceremonial proxy such

as a celebrant or employee of the funeral home witness the cremation.

- Currently 56 percent of all dispositions in the United States, projected to be 70 percent by 2030[22]
- Funeral pyres (outdoor cremations) are currently found only in Colorado; Maine is considering
- Remains may be interred in the ground or columbarium (crypt, niche, entombed), or ashes may be scattered, or the remains may be kept at home in a vessel
- Options are increasing to transform into plant material, keepsake, memorial spaceflight, coral reef, gems, etc.

Cryomation ("Promession")

- The body is freeze dried and crushed into particles afterwards
- This practice is not fully validated scientifically nor practically. Most information available comes directly from companies trying to create a fully functioning process rather than from independent review.

Donation to Science

- The entire body goes directly from the place of death to an academic or research organization
- Requests must be reviewed and approved by the accepting organization prior to death
- May or may not result in remains returning to the family at a later date

Natural Organic Reduction (NOR, Recomposition, Composting)

- No embalming or other chemicals are used
- Any toxic/non-natural implants or devices are removed
- Shrouding or casketing are in natural and biodegradable material
- Natural, organic reduction of the human body becomes usable soil in one to nine months.
- Washington State, Colorado, and Oregon recently made it legal; others are likely to follow. Legislation introduced in: Delaware, Hawaii, Maine, New York, and Vermont.

Sky Burial (Scaffolding, Tree Graves)
- Is occasionally practiced by some First People/Native Americans
- The body is arranged naked and open to the elements for exposure to animals and weather

SOME HELPFUL DATA

From most to least common in the United States (broadly speaking)
- Cremation - steadily increasing in popularity
- Conventional burial
- Green burial
- Donation to science
- Burial at sea
- Alkaline hydrolysis - will almost certainly become more common
- Recomposition - will almost certainly become more common

True environmental impact will be influenced by specific local conditions and environment, but the following is roughly from least to greatest environmental impact.
- Recomposition
- Green burial
- Donation to science
- Alkaline hydrolysis
- Cremation
- Conventional Burial
- Burial at Sea

These are averages, and will vary depending on region.
- Donation to Science $0, though a funeral may be held later
- Alkaline hydrolysis $1,000-2,500 for the process itself
- Cremation $1,000-2,500 for the process itself
- Green burial $2,500, may depend on type of land used
- Burial at Sea   Expensive, but less so for veterans
- Recomposition $5,500
- Conventional Burial $11,000, including plot and headstone

Who's Who in End-of-Life Services

The people and roles you may encounter, as well as what might be going on behind the scenes

The Dying

Someone who wants to plan their funeral or document ceremonial wishes before their death.

Concerns: This person has a number of concerns. They may have strong and changing feelings about this life phase. There is a decent chance they're meeting with you because they feel alone, have no one else to turn to, or they do not want to have these conversations with those close to them. Their primary concerns can run from control, urgency, and fear, to legacy, beauty, and meaning, to simplicity, cost and logistics.

In the United States, funeral homes are usually legally bound to follow the wishes of the legal Next of Kin or the person with the rights of disposition. Even if the deceased wrote down their preferences, the NoK can override those. But in many states it is possible to assign the rights of disposition to anyone you choose. These laws vary by state and are adjusted often.

If you have clients who are concerned that their wishes for death, dying, or ceremonies won't be respected, encourage them to appoint someone who is supportive of their wants, and to put it in a legal form that their state recognizes. For LGBTQ+ communities, this can be especially important due to concerns about names, gender identity, and gender expression being honored on legal forms and in ceremonies.[23]

Next of Kin (NoK) and/or person with rights of disposition

The person who has the legal right to direct the final disposition of the body. Generally, the plans for the funeral fall to them as well; however, in many families there will be a lot of collaboration of ideas and sharing of the workload. This person might be a legal representative of the deceased but not a family member or friend.

Concerns: This person is often most concerned with meeting any requests and wishes the deceased had, and perhaps especially concerned with carrying those out in the face of other family members who might not want the same thing. They are concerned with "doing the right thing" morally/ethically while in view of a number of other people (the family of origin, society, friends, etc.).

If they knew what the deceased wanted, they may have disagreed about ceremony aspects and are ambivalent about parts of the process or unsure how much to follow through on the wishes of the deceased. This person may also have legal Power of Attorney when it comes to financial decisions for the deceased, so there is often a financial component to their decisions. They may be managing a budget that includes not just the funeral, but all the affairs of the deceased.

Their emotions often depend on the manner and timing of the death of the deceased. Some NoK are relieved that the deceased is no longer suffering. Some had terrible relationships with the deceased and are angry that there is no hope of reconciliation or love coming from the deceased. Some are ashamed about the manner of death and wary about how to accomplish this somewhat public dance of ritual. Some will be deeply sad yet able to find a way to celebrate the life that has ended.

Spouses and partners of the dying or deceased

These may be the legal next of kin or not. They may have the rights of disposition or not. They may be legally recognized or not. They may have good relationships with the deceased's family of origin, or not. Generally, they are the NoK but some spouses discover they are not and it leads to interesting dynamics.

Concerns: Usually their concerns are the same as the NoK. In situations where they are not the legal NoK or with rights of disposition, there may be hurt feelings and jockeying for a voice.

Former spouses and partners of the deceased

These are somewhat self-explanatory. In places that allow common-law marriage, there might be different understandings between spouses and former spouses about their roles.

Concerns: Former spouses and partners may be concerned about feeling that they were a meaningful part, or any part, of the life story of the deceased. They might be concerned about being portrayed in a less than flattering role, or about seeing that the deceased led a much happier life after them. They may want to be included in decision making.

In general, none of this is your concern unless the NoK brings it up as an issue to be sensitive about. Legally you need to follow the wishes of the person with rights of disposition. But it is best to be frank and transparent when you learn of former spouses and families: "Is there a role for members of that family that would feel appropriate to you?" If there are concerns about acting out during the ceremony, sometimes you can give former spouses and families nominal but formal roles so they feel included.

Primary mourners

The primary mourners include the immediate family and/or close friends. This cluster of people will vary depending on the age and family constellations of the deceased. It may be parents, siblings, and grandparents. It may be a spouse and children. In situations where the deceased does not have many friends or family alive, it may be a caregiver from hospice or a nursing home.

Concerns: Generally, primary mourners are concerned about feeling at sea during the various motions and moments of the ceremony. They are usually dealing with strong emotions, and sometimes with competing emotions. They want to know what they are supposed to do next. They want the day to go smoothly and clarity about what will happen. They may feel scrutinized or detached.

Funeral director (FD), funeral home employees (pallbearers, drivers, ushers), cemetery employees, and grounds crew

Generally, the funeral home's lead employee on site is a FD. Funeral homes can have multiple FDs; it is essentially a level of employment. They can make decisions in the moment if things need to change, for instance bringing the hearse around sooner, or communicating with the grounds crew if the ceremony runs long. Fundamentally they are responsible for the arrival of the body of the deceased to the funeral, the entrance and placement of the deceased at the place of the ceremony, and the recession or exit of the body to its next stop toward final disposition.

Concerns: FDs want everything to run smoothly. In my experience they are generally unflappable. You would never know by looking at them that something was not going as planned. They are usually very experienced and very calm. If they have hired you, they want a celebrant who reflects what the family wants and needs, but who also reflects well on them.

Cemetery employees will want to know that you understand their particular policies and that you're ready and prepared to deliver the ceremony service. You will interact with grounds crew during a graveside committal service, coordinating the lowering of the casket, the burying of the urn, or the closing of a niche. For some burials of urns, there is no grounds crew around and they will do it after the mourners leave. Before lowering caskets, the grounds crew usually stands off to the side at a respectful distance.

Roles and Responsibilities of the End-of-Life Celebrant

The celebrant takes on different skills and roles at different times in the process. Above all, families want to know that they are doing this important, unfamiliar thing "correctly." Is it enough? Is it good enough? At each step you can do them a service by **validating their choices** and reassuring them that those choices fall in the social scheme of appropriateness.

Some families want you to provide guidance while they collaborate on the service. Others will want you to do everything within your scope because they have no energy or interest in creating the service. They need to store up their energy to simply attend the funeral. Be prepared to sensitively ask where your client/family may fall on this continuum and give them permission to be along the spectrum.

Families also need to know that someone is in charge of the ceremony so they can shift gears from administering the grief process, to participating in it. Knowing that you are leading the ceremony allows them to turn more toward grief and memory. For a few days, you may be the primary connection between the family and the funeral home. If you encounter logistical needs like microphones, flowers, small tables, etc., you can run the list by the FD to ensure they can be provided or remind the family to follow through on this need.

Families need to **trust you and build rapport** quickly. My experience has been that whatever I can do to be transparent about who I am and what I will do, helps. Along with letting the family know that I am a professional, able to roll with the chaos they are in, and that they are in good hands, I also let them know that their choices are very open, and that whatever is done with love and positive intention will generally turn out just fine. I also give them permission to make mis-steps. You can say things like, "If you haven't done this before, let me tell you that there are always things that seem to get missed and are very fluid. That's just the way it is. If you encounter changes, know that it is normal." This helps reduce stress and anxiety at a moment-by-moment level.

Be a creative source for ways to express their love and duty of care. Look for opportunities for ceremony, from a few words, to small ritual gestures, to multi-part ceremonies. These are the "beats" of the event that will help the bereaved find their places in it. Be aware that small moments of just being present with each other can be among the most helpful, meaningful, and easiest "rituals" to include.

Advocate for the choices of the Next of Kin. Let the NoK know that their choices are well and good. When there are disagreements (you may or may not be present for them) use your judgment about the prevailing needs of the family as opposed to the choices of the NoK to help forge compromises or new solutions. If there are difficult relationships, you can look for or create small "honor roles" for those difficult people to appease them and take the heat from the Next of Kin.

Lastly, a celebrant often needs to **tenderly nudge family members and loved ones into the physical acts and emotional spaces** that open up during end-of-life ceremonies and rituals. This is usually as simple as saying, "And now would you step forward and lay your flowers on Margaret's final place of rest?" But sometimes it is coaching ahead of time. "Yes, a committal is difficult, but everyone I know who has held a funeral for a loved one has said that it felt like one of the most important moments." You can also be their proxy for some of the most difficult things: reading a tribute if someone is crying too much, or leading the casket out of the ceremony space if the primary mourner cannot.

RESPONSIBILITIES

You will not always do everything in the ceremony, but you will be overseeing these basics and doing what you can to make sure events go to plan. You are responsible for:

- overall ceremony design, flow, and materials list;
- being aware of the position and movement of the body during the ceremony, and understanding what will happen when, and by whom;
- interfacing with the funeral home, cemetery, and/or ceremony location for logistical needs and materials, and especially keeping providers in the loop on choices the family makes;
- facilitating, emceeing, and generally keeping the ceremony on track, which might include adjusting the program if things change part way through, as well as checking in with participants about whether they are prepared for their portion of the ceremony;
- writing and delivering opening words that set the tone, let people what is happening, and provide some meaning;
- writing and delivering a eulogy, or identifying others who will deliver it;
- creating or suggesting rituals if requested and if you sense they would be helpful;
- suggesting, finding, and/or reading poems or other meaningful written work;
- suggesting music;
- writing and delivering the commendation, the most formal goodbye on behalf of all present;
- closing words that reassure mourners they have honored their loved one, and giving them support and fortitude;
- ending the ceremony and dismissing the participants and guests; and
- the committal service.

The Variety of End-of-Life Ceremonies

Commemorative ceremonies from dying days to anniversary dates

More than any other ceremony type, end-of-life services are varied. As mentioned previously, the kinds of funeral ceremonies most common in one region of the country may differ from ones in other areas. As a nation, we are definitely seeing an increase in cremation as a disposition. For most parts of the country, the common ceremonies or sets of ceremonies you will encounter are:

- a complete "full length" funeral with cremated remains present, sometimes followed by an ash scattering or inurnment committal service;
- a short graveside ceremony to bury a casket or urn, without a full funeral;
- a complete funeral ceremony with casketed remains, held in a funeral home, church, or other space, followed by a graveside (or *committal*) service or cremation;
- a celebration of life ceremony with the body present in some way; and
- a memorial service, with no remains present, held after the final disposition or committal.

In addition to formal ceremonies, there are "opportunities for ceremony" when ceremonial gestures might be appreciated and appropriate.[24] Ceremony gestures are small moments that acknowledge the emotional experiences of the grieving. A gesture is usually brief and simple: a sentence, a moment of silence, the chime of a bell, laying a hand on the casket or shroud, wearing a special color, or something equally minimal and sensory. You may encounter opportunities for these gestures if you are involved in activities aside from the formal funeral service. Different families, different choices, different emotional waves, different times will call for different responses on your part as a celebrant.

Marking these moments will set you apart from the average or inexperienced celebrant, and shows a level of sensitivity to what families are going through. Some examples of when you might use a gesture are:

- when the body changes states of being, changes location, or changes hands, for example if you're present when ashes are delivered from the Funeral Director (FD) to a family member;
- when remains of the deceased interact with fire, water, air, or earth; and
- moments when the bereaved might feel vulnerable, unsure, or concerned they are doing the right thing in how they are handling the deceased.

Below is a list of the different kinds of end-of-life ceremonies you will likely encounter.

Living Wake - Living Funeral

These terms are often used interchangeably. A living wake is a gathering to honor, toast, love, cherish, and say goodbye directly to someone who is going to die imminently, and usually who is still mentally aware enough to appreciate the event. The dying person is almost always the one who requests this sort of gathering, whether it is a last meal together, a party, or simple goodbyes. This person may seek a celebrant to create the event so that it is meaningful, manageable, and has elements of ritual.

Home Vigil

A home vigil is a gathering around a loved one just before or immediately after death. A little bit of ritual and ceremony at this time can help people punctuate their understanding that this person is about to die or has died. Holding hands around the bed, reading aloud from a favorite book, saying poems, moments of silence, lighting a candle, opening windows, addressing the person with goodbyes, anointing or dressing the dying, placing flowers, or singing are ways you might mark this threshold.

Deathbed Rituals

These are small rituals that can be done immediately after death, no matter where the death occurs. Examples could be washing the body, shrouding, lighting a candle, singing a mourning song or a favorite song of the deceased, reading a poem, or giving a benediction.

Movement of the Body

A short phrase or ritual can help the bereaved when the body of the deceased is moved, whether it is from room to room (e.g., from a bedroom to a living room for home funeral), from a private room in a care facility to a holding room, or from the place of death into a vehicle for transport to a funeral home or crematorium. You would not stretch out these moments and mark all of them, but even just putting a hand on the casket for a few seconds and taking a breath can help you and the family remain present and embodied enough to continue through the necessary events of the day.

Home Funeral

Families in every state in the United States may keep the deceased at home or bring them home.[25] Families can participate in very traditional rituals like cleaning and dressing the body, preparing it for viewing, decorating the room where the person will lie in honor, and moving the body for the last time from the places where it lived. A funeral home or family member will later transport the body to a funeral home, crematorium, or burial ground.

Direct Cremation

The body is removed from the place of death by a funeral home director or family member and transported directly to the crematorium for cremation. Sometimes families may want someone like a celebrant present at a cremation, even if they themselves choose not to be. Many times, a family does not know they are allowed to have a ceremony for cremation, or can choose witnessed cremation as an option.

Direct Burial

For direct burials, the only formal ceremony will be at the grave site, either at the time of burial or at a later date. There is no viewing/visitation/wake or complete ceremony at a location other than the grave. Remains are usually not embalmed or arranged for viewing. A direct burial may also refer to the burial of an urn of cremated remains. In either case, the only time for a formal ceremony is at the burial site.

Movement of the Body to and from the Ceremony

The more formal the event, the more "punctuation" there will be at various steps of the progress of the body. Opportunities for ceremony may be: before the body is removed from the visitation room, as the body is received by a vehicle, as the body is removed from a vehicle, when pallbearers are fully supporting the body, when the body crosses the threshold of the ceremony space, when the body is placed in its ceremony position, when it is taken up by pallbearers, when it crosses the threshold in leaving the ceremony space, when it is received by a vehicle, when it arrives at the site of final disposition. Again, you would not interrupt the flow by using gestures for all of these moves, but using a gesture judiciously can help those grieving stay present and add moments of respect for the deceased.

Viewing (also called a visitation, wake, or calling hours)

Viewings do not have a strong ceremonial aspect. Simply being there, in the presence of the deceased, is the ritual. They are a time to confront the physical reality of death and come together as a community to cope. A celebrant might be involved in opening and closing the time.

Funeral Service

The funeral service is the primary ceremony held after death to acknowledge death and honor the life of the deceased. To distinguish it from other ceremonies, I feel that if the body is present in some form, then it is a funeral service. Some ceremonies will be minimalist, and others will be maximalist. It depends on the preferences of the family and the ability to pull it off. Some deaths will have no funeral service but only a committal, which might have the feel of a hybrid funeral-committal.

Green Burial (also called natural burial, conservation burial, or hybrid cemetery burial)

Green burials resemble traditional funeral services in that they are a "full length" ceremony, but instead of the remains being enclosed in a casket of manmade or non-biodegradable materials, the remains are shrouded only in natural fibers or in a wood or paper casket. Ceremonially, there may be some unique elements to pay attention to, such as the very choice to be buried naturally, the procession of the body from transport to the site (most conservation lands do not allow motorized vehicles), and rituals that reference and include environmental elements–especially elements right at the gravesite.

Committal Service (also called a graveside service or the final disposition)

These ceremonies mark the transformational moments when the body changes form for its very last time, or when the family or friends will never again be with this body in its physical form. A graveside service is where the casket or urn is buried or enclosed. A witnessed cremation is when the body is viewed as it moves into the crematory retort. An ash scattering is when the cremated remains are returned to the elements. These are all committal services. They are usually not longer than thirty minutes and may be closer to five or fifteen minutes if there has been a prior ceremony.

Online Funeral

There are two main types of online funerals: those that stream a funeral service where the body is present in some form, and those hosted as a gathering when the body is not present due to some circumstance, but the stated purpose of the gathering is to hold a funeral. During the Covid-19 pandemic both kinds of services became common. For streaming ceremonies, the capability is usually found with specific funeral homes or cemeteries. For online gatherings, many celebrants found ways during the pandemic to create their own online spaces via video conferencing technologies.

Witnessed Cremation

Witnessed cremation ceremonies are services created around the act of moving the body into the crematory retort. Many cemeteries with a crematorium are now creating beautiful, chapel-like settings for witnessed cremation ceremonies. In countries and places where cremation rates are high, a witnessed cremation service may be the most common service.

Ash Scattering

An ash scattering ceremony occurs days, weeks, or months after the body has been cremated. Ash scattering ceremonies are sometimes governed by state or local laws, so it is helpful to look into what the rules are in your area, or at local places that might appeal to families.

Memorial Service

A "true" memorial service is a ceremony or event where the body is not present. Memorials might be held days, months, or years after a committal. They often bring together extended communities that were impacted by the life of the deceased. Usually there has already been a funeral service, even if it was very brief or basic. Often these are upbeat and feel more like a celebration of life than a funeral.

When you get an inquiry for a memorial, ask if there has already been a funeral and when it was. If there has not been one, you will need to be sensitive to whether the family is asking for what they really need, or if there is a confusion about terms. If there has not been a funeral yet and the body will be present, then consider it a funeral, at least in terms of purpose, design, elements, and pricing. Even if it is happening long after the disposition and is going to have a celebratory tone, it is the first time they will be ritualizing the death. That can bring different elements and emotions to the mix.

Communal or Mass Memorials

Many research institutions have communal ceremonies to thank and honor those who donated their bodies to science, and the families of the deceased are often invited. Organizations like nursing homes have ceremonies for Mother's Day or Father's Day to honor those who died in the previous year. And, of course, there are ceremonies for military veterans, for pets, for pandemics, and other events where there is a sense of community and communal responsibility. Generally, these are held annually at a municipal or institutional level to memorialize all those who have died in the previous year.

Milestone Dates

Some families have small ceremonies, essentially memorial ceremonies, on important dates. Some examples are on Father's Day if their dad died that year, a birthday of a child who died, the death anniversary of a parent, the anniversary of a date a beloved pet died.

Infant Death, Deaths of Possibility

Some people experience a miscarriage, or who suffer stillbirth or crib death of their infant, want to mark the loss and are helped by moving through the formal motions of a funeral. There are different considerations for each of these groups, and each survivor or family will bring its own specific meaning and emotional realities to the event.

Celebration of Life

A convergence of trends and demographics are shifting the ideas that many people have about the purpose of a funeral. Rather than only mourning and grieving, people are increasingly choosing to mark the death of a family member or friend by emphasizing their joy that this person lived, their gratitude at knowing the deceased, and by celebrating the universal and specific traits of the deceased.

A celebration of life may describe the tone of the funeral, or it might describe the type of event. The most common differentiator is the presence of a body or human remains in any form. If there will be remains present, it is best to treat the event as a funeral whose tone is upbeat, bringing out the happiness of the attendees for knowing the deceased. If no remains will be present, you can treat the event more like a memorial. In either case, celebrations of life often take place in venues or locations deeply personal to the deceased or reflective of their accomplishments. There may be a desire for family photographs, "roasting" the deceased, and generally pivoting to joy quite early in the program.

In determining what the event is, it is best to be direct and explicit with the family or planners. Ask if there was already a funeral. Ask if the remains of the deceased will be present. Ask if there is a level of celebration or joy that would be "too much" for them, so you have some idea about the emotional range of what you are creating and conducting.

LOOKING AHEAD

Direct cremation with or without a ceremony, direct burials with a ceremony, and natural burials are quickly becoming the most preferred dispositions, and therefore the most requested ceremonies that individuals and families seek. The interest is likely a combination of cost, values, family distance, and the pandemic. As you set out to create ceremonies that will satisfy the people and communities in your area, making sure you include these ceremony types may allow you to be more creative, to appeal to a wider range of clients, and to discover new colleagues and professionals in your area.

It remains to be seen if online or streamed funeral services will continue, out of need or convenience, after the current pandemic. However, more than half of all NFDA-member funeral homes now offer some sort of online component to funeral services.[26] This is likely to grow. This book's final chapter, *The Future of Funerals*, talks more about trends in end-of-life care and ceremonies, including the integration of technology and virtual spaces.

Part 2.
Funeral Design

Funeral Design

While funeral ceremonies are varied and diverse, there are five major concepts that shape their design. They are similar to other ceremonies, and if you have experience as a celebrant they will be familiar: tone, meaning, beliefs, stories, and ritual/symbolism. Your ceremonies should take all of these concepts into account.

TONE - GUIDING THE ELEMENTS AND MAKING ROOM FOR FEELINGS

Most end-of-life ceremonies encompass a range of emotions, from sadness to joy to peace. Most "typical" funerals begin on a sad note, reach their lowest emotional point around the commendation and, if possible, turn toward hope, resolution, or acceptance. Even though the funeral shouldn't try to change the emotions or grief of the primary mourners, it does present them with a miniature version of an overall emotional journey, from shock or sadness to full integration of the reality of death. The tone of the funeral is a combination of the emotional arc and the level of formality of the service. You might get a request for a highly formal service that is intensely joyful, or a request for a relaxed service that is full of despair.

Tone will drive many decisions, from where to have the ceremony, what rituals to include, who will speak, the music, readings, and more. Identifying the tone will make your decisions easier, and one of the first things I do as an end-of-life celebrant is try to pin it down. It is trickier than with other ceremonies. If you get the tone wrong, you risk jostling the family out of step with their feelings. Try to get comfortable confirming it in some way directly with the family. Often I ask something such as, "When you think back on the day of the funeral, what are a few things you hope about it?"

Over time, I've come to see the ceremony tone falling into a few categories. The terms below are placeholders only, based on the ceremonies I've officiated over the years. Ceremonies in your area or communities may have a very different range. Do not get too attached to the terms; communicate with the NoK for their feelings and concepts.

Formal and stately — This is what you might see for the funeral of an older, established person who had a number of "elder" roles in the community. It is a ceremony often used to confirm status, honor, or inspiration. Usually it has a number of rituals and elements carried out with attention to form. Mourning practices might amplify or exaggerate the community's well-established forms and rituals.

Sincere and solemn — This kind of ceremony includes more personal notes than a formal funeral. It is focused on support, community, pulling together, and getting through. These ceremonies are structured, but not overly choreographed, and have room for participation. Expressions of grief are usually personal and raw.

Thoughtful and participatory — This ceremony engages the mind and uses language, senses, and reflective silences combined with participation and spontaneous elements. It can be difficult for a celebrant to manage a service with loose or spontaneous elements. Without some more formal elements, the ceremony can feel like a team-building event. Consider having symbolic opening and closing rituals or gestures.

Relaxed and appreciative — This is a very common tone for funerals for the expected deaths of people who have lived long and happy lives. Feelings of appreciation and acceptance come to the foreground. Most funerals that are celebrations of life fall into this category. There is a sense that the community's "normal" ceremony structure is correct and adequate, and that the tone will be generally positive.

Unconventional, alternative — This kind of ceremony strives to take control of the narrative of death, playing with the form of the service in some way. Expressions of grief might be unconventional, creative, darkly humorous, or channeled into other emotions. The setting might be unusual. When creating something highly innovative, a few predictable elements may be needed to help the ceremony move along an emotional arc.

MEANING - FINDING OR MAKING IT

Finding or making meaning from the life of the deceased and sharing it through the ceremony helps mourners offset the shocking absence of their loved one. It cannot take the place of their physical presence, but highlighting the specifics of a life gives mourners something in its stead. It is a lackluster swap, but one that the bereaved will make more frequently now. Therefore, it is important to understand what gave the deceased purpose, where they found meaning, what they thought was most important in making this journey from birth to death. This is the basis for writing the eulogy, which aims to paint an accurate image of the deceased and elevate their specific life choices and events into something universally valued. The meaning is found in those universal values.

Occasionally, you will encounter deceased who believed very strongly in one or more of the humanist prongs of life and lived their life in service: someone utterly devoted to research science in infectious disease; someone who worked tirelessly for LGBTQ+ protections; someone who expressed the human condition through art. These can easily be incorporated into a message of meaning.

BELIEFS - ELICITING AND AFFIRMING THEM

As a nonreligious celebrant, you will have some clues about the outlook of the deceased and/or their next of kin by the fact that you are the one performing the service. However, too often I find that the religious and nonreligious both think a funeral for those without belief in a god is doubly difficult. The thought is, not only has a loved one died, but the bereaved must now also suffer that death without even the support of a belief system or promise of an afterlife.

As humanist or nonreligious celebrants, we have a responsibility to show that a world filled with this Earth's nature, the capacity of the human mind, the bold adventure of science, the creation of a system of ethics seeking equality, justice, peace, and harmony for all beings—all this before we even get to love, companionship, care for others, fun, art, neighborliness, self-sacrifice, and compassion—that this world is as comforting, hopeful, supportive, and compelling as a world in which there is a god or an afterlife. Maybe even more so because it already surrounds us and we are already members of it.

You can also seek to understand the beliefs of the primary mourners and include those in the ceremony. If the beliefs of the deceased were in contrast to the beliefs of those closest to them, it's ok to acknowledge that, and then move forward in some way that affirms the value of both.

STORIES AND CREATIVE WRITING - KEEPING PEOPLE ENGAGED

This is where the rubber hits the road, so to speak. Everything you have understood about the deceased and their constellation of experiences is crystallized into stories. There is more detail in the section on eulogies—what stories to select, how to organize multiple stories, how to write your story of the deceased—but the main point is that we humans have evolved to enjoy, invest meaning in, and be comforted by the structure of stories. Tell ones that keep these mourners involved emotionally.

RITUALS AND SYMBOLS - BYPASSING THE MIND

Rituals are a combination of meaning and the senses. They heighten an experience and keep us in our bodies at a time when that may be difficult. Experiences that involve multiple senses reside more strongly and deeply in us. Rituals also short-circuit the thinking mind to evoke emotion. And finally, they mark this time as special, unusual, extra-ordinary, alongside our regular flow of time and activities. You will incorporate meaningful rituals and formal rituals to give your ceremonies nuance and sinew.

There are two things it is probably helpful to mention here. One is that, for the most part, there will not be anything very special or momentous about the people you are creating funerals for. They are usually not celebrities, nor special in their towns, not particularly successful in their fields, not always successful in the relationships of their lives. The funeral is not meant to prop them up as someone more special than they were. The funeral is about finding the unique characteristics that will be missed, and connecting those characteristics to universal themes, which will give the bereaved fortitude for the coming weeks, months, and years.

Second, although this book focuses in depth on the different design elements that go into funerals, do not over-complicate the ceremony. More often than not, it is the simple gestures, rituals, and eulogies that are the most meaningful. A complex funeral, with complicated themes, stuffed with rituals, music, and readings is not a better funeral. Keep in mind that mourners might not remember that the specifics of the day were "So unique!" They will remember that they had the funeral.

Typical Funeral Ceremony Elements

"Typical" is an intentionally broad term. Much of what we think of as typical for funerals has trickled down from widely reported white, Anglican funerals[27] and then been perpetuated via mass media. In the United States, the funerals of Abraham Lincoln[28] in 1865 and Queen Victoria[29] in 1901 significantly influenced today's funeral and customs, along with Victorian practices surrounding death, such as mourning clothes and mortuary accessories. Abraham Lincoln's funeral was influential because it depended so heavily on embalming, and created a sense of American pomp that wealthy Americans went on to imitate. Therefore, keep in mind the origins of these elements and treat them as *possible* ingredients in the funerals you are creating rather than requirements. Given the diversity of the United States, they may not represent the funeral traditions of even most of the cultures you will serve.

LENGTH OF CEREMONIES

In my area, full-length funeral ceremonies are about sixty minutes long. It is not clear to me why one hour is the norm, but most people arranging a funeral have a sense that it is a correct and respectable length of time. I believe it is a holdover from the weekly religious observances, and is inherited from those traditions.

After the family meeting, I round up or down based on what they have in mind. Longer ceremonies can work in cases where the deceased was older, led a full life, died uneventfully, and/or had a large family. Traumatic deaths and premature deaths, on the other hand, can leave families drained by a ceremony longer than about thirty minutes. As an example, I have led fifteen-minute graveside services for someone who died by suicide, and three-hour chapel services for a long-lived person with multiple generations from many countries. If the ceremony I am creating looks like it will be shorter than thirty minutes or longer than one hour, I usually give the NoK some notice so we're in agreement before the day of the service. I explain my thinking about why the ceremony works or doesn't work at the length we have.

The ceremony length may also be determined by cost, and you should feel fine about asking the NoK and/or FD outright whether there is a planned end time, especially if you sense the family envisions something complex.

MOVEMENT OF THE BODY

The movement of the body carries with it a significant symbolism of the beginning and ending of the ceremony. It is also what most mourners and celebrants are the most awkward about. So, be clear for yourself about where the body will be during different parts of the ceremony. Will it be brought in by pall bearers, before, after, or with the primary mourners? Will there be an urn in place before guests arrive? Will it be brought in after them? There is no right and wrong, but it is important to have a high level of clarity for the family's peace of mind. With cremated remains it is also important to know what will happen to the vessel after the ceremony. Will someone take it home? Will it be buried by the FD later?

A COMPLETE FUNERAL CEREMONY

The elements below often occur in neutral nonreligious ceremony spaces like funeral homes or non-denominational chapels. The order of elements is open to interpretation and need, and elements sometimes overlap in the cases of multimedia or sensory elements. Elements can and should be adjusted if the needs of your particular ceremony call for it. Keep in mind that most ceremonies will not include *all* these elements. Sometimes even the ceremony setting will limit whether some elements can be used. When referred to as a whole, the elements for a ceremony are called the Order of Service (OOS).

Music – Background music may be used to set the tone of the ceremony, reflect the personality of the deceased or, when it is paused, to symbolize the beginning of the ceremony. Other music may follow on directly to mark the opening of the ceremony.

Entrance and positioning of the body – This may happen before the arrival of family or with the family's entrance. Some common versions:

- A casket is positioned at the front of the ceremony space by funeral home employees before guests arrive and family enter.
- An urn is positioned at the front of the ceremony space by funeral home employees or a family member before guests arrive and family enter.
- A casket is carried in by pallbearers and followed by the primary mourners after guests have been seated.
- An urn is brought in after guests have been seated, carried by a designated mourner and followed by the primary mourners.
- Less frequently, the guests and primary mourners are seated and the casket or urn is brought in by the funeral director.

Arrival of guests – Guests tend to arrive on the early side for a funeral, sometimes up to an hour before the ceremony starts. There may also be a viewing before the formal start of the ceremony, which can prevent you from setting up if you arrive during that time. If you have complicated sound or setup needs, check in with the NoK about when they plan to arrive and adjust your timing accordingly.

Rituals for guests on arrival – Guests can participate in small rituals, such as receiving a flower, looking at photo books, watching a slideshow, or signing a guestbook. These small elements count as rituals in my opinion, but they may be an intentional part of the ceremony or someone may have set it up with the FD outside of the formal bounds of the funeral ceremony. If you have specific, planned rituals (for instance, everyone taking a seed packet in memory of a gardener) you may need to formalize these a bit more with signage or announcements to clarify their purpose.

Housekeeping announcement – These announcements take place before primary mourners arrive (turn off phones, availability of assistive hearing options, etc.).

Formal start to the ceremony – Include something that announces the start of the ceremony or the entrance of the primary mourners, and adds another layer of "beginning" to the ceremony. This can be anything from lighting a candle to chiming a bell to lighting incense or placing the urn in the place of honor and laying flowers nearby. Use an element that makes sense for the ceremony you are creating.

Entrance of primary mourners – In my experience there is usually not much standing-sitting-standing at humanist funerals. Before the funeral, the family is often taking advantage of the time to talk with guests, and everyone simply finds their seats when you announce the ceremony is starting. But any formal entrance of the family, especially if they are carrying the urn or accompanying or preceding the body in any way, would be a good place to ask people to stand as they are able.

Instructions to family and guests – This is to let people know things like whether there is a time in the ceremony for shared stories, a reception afterward, or that the primary mourners will not be available after the ceremony. I find there is no great place for this at the beginning of the ceremony. It really breaks the emotional start of the ceremony. You can put much of it in the housekeeping announcement before the ceremony starts. And other elements can be shared after the main parts of the ceremony, but before the closing message/benediction. After you have written your full ceremony, review to see if this element is in the appropriate place.

Opening Words – Opening words are usually composed of a few elements: a welcome, housekeeping notes, introduction, affirmation, and intention. If you introduce yourself, it is often couched in language that you are honored to conduct this ceremony on behalf of the family of the deceased. (Use their names when you say it.) You will learn more about these terms in greater detail in the section on the written framework.

Acknowledging those unable to attend or who have died already – When important family or friends are unable to attend, it is helpful to call them to mind, as a way of bringing even more love and support to the primary mourners. It is also a way to expand the meaning of this person's death, or to symbolically expand the "attendees," by placing the deceased in their lineage of those who have already died.

Thank you to the funeral home, director, other professionals – This is considered good form. The family is often too overwhelmed to think of this, but grateful you do it. It also tends to build good relationships between celebrants and other end-of-life professionals.

Pause – It helps the pacing and emotional milestones of the ceremony if you pause at some key moments. I like a pause after all of the introductory components. It helps bring back people who have already checked out. It helps you manage your breathing, posture, and performance. It helps refocus on an important part of the ceremony.

Reading the obituary – This practice started at a time when fewer people were literate. The obituary was read during the ceremony so that all those present had the same details about the life and death of the deceased. Some families continue to ask for this element, but usually because they think it is something they are supposed to include. I do not think it accomplishes much in terms of ceremony, so if a family asks for it I try to uncover why. Sometimes a family member has put a lot of effort into writing it. If it doesn't serve the ceremony, perhaps it could be printed and shared as a handout. If you have a funeral that is very sparse for some reason, or attended by a large number of people who did not know the deceased at all, you also might consider including it.

Celebrant message – This is very freeform and will vary greatly depending on the beliefs of the deceased and family, your personal style, the requests of the family, and the personality of the deceased. You can think of it like the "sermon" piece of a religious ceremony. You are mixing your personal outlook (they have hired you because it overlaps enough with their own) with the specifics of this family and this person who has died. It can lean heavily on excerpts from art or sport or music or video games or hobbies of the deceased. It can be utterly somber, or stirring, or funny. It is really up to you to use your skills to elicit what the family needs, bring in your creative juices, and craft something.

Message about death (based on the life stance of the deceased or primary mourners) – This is sometimes a standalone section, more direct than the previous celebrant message, because it leads right into the eulogies. It is a way to "remind" the family and bereaved of their beliefs, or of the beliefs of the deceased, before hearing the life story of their loved one. Sometimes it is combined with the celebrant message.

Formal eulogy – The life story of this person who lived with us on earth and is no longer embodied here, giving this life a beginning, middle, and end, calling attention to the shining moments of a life, the real moments of a life, the challenges of a life, in order to view it as a complete and whole thing. The formal eulogy might be given by one person or shared by many. It might be given by the celebrant, or others. It doesn't have to be a linear chronology.

Planned tributes/remembrances – Participation from family and friends or notable connections to give even more depth and breadth to the life story. They allow people present to understand this life as a whole, in addition to the slice they may have seen most often.

Moment of silence – A pause to reground, reembody ourselves in the face of loss, or to say our own private message in the middle of a difficult event. Symbolically represents the absence of the deceased.

Readings, poems, music, art, and quotes (might also be displayed rather than spoken) – Our world is reflected and improved on by artists, writers, and musicians. They represent some of the best parts of humanity. These elements put into words and images things we may have trouble expressing, and can amplify the messages we are sharing. They also make the funeral "more special." Music especially can make it easier for us to express emotions that feel too scary out on their own, and can help organize (and soothe) emotions that are overwhelming us. These elements can be placed throughout the ceremony where it makes sense. Use them as punctuation, or emotional onramps and offramps, for where we are in the ceremony.

Singing – A frequent difference between religious and nonreligious funerals is the absence of singing in nonreligious funerals; however, singing is a wonderful "community ritual" on a lot of levels. One, it can help the primary mourners feel surrounded physically by their community. Two, it is participatory and keeps people engaged emotionally in the ceremony. And three (perhaps most beneficial), it is a stress relief technique because it requires deep breathing and regular pacing.

Photo slideshow or other multimedia experience – Despite the number of photos we take on our phones these days, photos of the ones we love are still special. They crystalize the joyful, intimate, vulnerable, and special moments of our life. Personally, I believe that photos, video, and other visual representations of the deceased also let the bereaved "rest" their eyes and psyches from looking at the remains of their loved one. The bereaved are in a limbo and, while here, they regard both versions of the deceased.

Art/Craft/Hobby representations of the deceased – This is a way to personalize the ceremony by using elements of the life of the deceased and how they spent their time. If the deceased was an artist or maker of any sort, this is also a great way to survey their work, their life, and one of the ways they have impacted the world. For instance, if they were in a band, their band might play a song.

A photographer might have photos displayed. A hockey fan might have t-shirts and hats from their favorite team.

Spontaneous tributes/remembrances – This is a time set aside when anyone present can share a story or anecdote or tribute to the deceased. As the celebrant, you need to keep an eye on whether there is enough time to include them, and you sometimes need to manage a microphone and speaking times to make sure people do not run long.

Celebrant transitions – These are all the little phrases that allow you to move smoothly from one element to another, from (for instance) when Aunt Coco gets up to talk about the favorite dish of the deceased and then a friend plays a rendition of Dark Side of the Moon. I will often thank people for sharing, use it as an example of some larger quality or characteristic of the deceased, and then pivot to the next element.

Commendation –This is a direct address to the deceased, where you literally turn to the bodily remains and acknowledge quite plainly that they have died and we are relinquishing them to death. If you are not moving directly to a graveside committal service after the funeral, it can help to put this element here.

Closing ritual – Often there is a reversal or "undoing" of the opening ritual that acts as a formal/final goodbye gesture for the primary mourners. If they lit candles on arrival, they might now blow them out. If they laid quilts across the casket, they might now fold them up.

Closing words – Preparing for the last moments of the ceremony, and adding another brief message about the life of the deceased, Humanism, and what we hold dear that will support us in the coming weeks, months, and year.

Instructions to family and guests – Here is where you again let people know what is going to happen immediately afterwards, and what they should do right now. Many people are very unsure what to do at this point so it is very helpful to give them guidance. For instance, "The pallbearers will now bring Jim's body out from our service, and the family will follow directly afterward. Please let them exit first so they can walk directly behind. Thank you." If there is a graveside committal service, or an ash scattering, or a witnessed cremation you can let people know it is optional, and give them a chance to slip away politely.

Dismissal – In addition to the closing words, funerals very often need the celebrant to clearly state the ceremony is over. This is a critical moment releasing the family from their duty and giving them permission to leave. "You have expressed your love and honored the life of Carter. Our ceremony is now over, please go in peace."

Receiving line of family – This depends on whether there will be a graveside service directly following or not, and where, and on whether the family would like to do it. The receiving line can work well after the ceremony, by telling guests that the family will exit first, then directing the family to line up at the exit, and then guests file out. For a graveside service, when it has ended, you can ask guests to form two lines to create an aisle through which the family can depart first. This gives people something to do, is ritualistic, and signals the end of this ceremony decisively.

Recession of the body – The exit of the body from the ceremony space. Generally, the pallbearers withdraw with the body, and the family files out directly behind the casket. If you have an urn and are going to a committal service, identify who is going to take the urn and they can exit the service first, with the family following. If it is very casual, people might start mingling and the urn can stay at the front of the ceremony space until the family takes it to the reception. The main point is to be clear with yourself and with the primary mourners what is going to happen with the body. How it is going to move, who is going to do that, and when?

Filler – It is helpful to have a reading or two of just a few sentences in case the funeral director or cemetery staff need to coordinate things at moments of transition. Perhaps a passage from the deceased's favorite book or song. I've used text from video games and Magic the Gathering, as well as my own library of poems.

Main Written Parts of the Ceremony

Funeral ceremonies have much more written—and therefore, spoken—material by the celebrant than most ceremonies. These are the parts of the ceremony that are your responsibility to write and deliver unless others volunteer. Whether your ceremony is sixty minutes or ten minutes, it is helpful to punctuate the shape of the service with the following elements in some form.

OPENING WORDS

Opening words get people settled and focus them toward the emotional task of the day. Here, you will also let people know how things will proceed. Your funeral may be the first funeral some people have ever attended and there is great concern about "doing the right thing." The main ingredients for the opening are a **welcome**, any **housekeeping**, an **affirmation**, and an **intention**. The order of these can be changed. You can eliminate one or more depending on the service. You can add items. But overall you want to thank people for coming, set the tone, name the purpose of the gathering, and let people know what they need to do and when. Here is the function each of these parts plays in the opening:

Welcome and Housekeeping – State a brief welcome and introduction. Before you start in earnest it is good to remind people to turn off their phones and notifications. When you introduce yourself, it is often couched in language expressing that you are a celebrant and that you are honored to conduct this ceremony on behalf of the family. Sometimes I place the welcome and housekeeping before the symbolic start of the service, so that the emotional and ceremonial flow are not interrupted by logistical information.

It is generally good form to thank, on behalf of the family, the funeral home and/or cemetery workers, as well as any notable doctors, hospitals, or hospices that helped care for the deceased. It is also helpful to orient guests to what this ceremony will be like. If it is a completely nonreligious ceremony, give some context about that. Also, tell people what they will do at each step, such as "We will honor Aliyah's life, then we'll have a short walk to the burial site where all can join There's a reception at The Bowlarama afterwards hosted so kindly by Aliyah's friends. There will be time in the ceremony to share memories."

Affirmation - This is a short message affirming the value of life, human life, and our humanity in general. It checks one of the boxes of the purposes of the funeral, which is to remind ourselves that we are human, to place ourselves in the vastness of space and time, and to connect to the universality of death and change. We are singular in missing and mourning this person. We join all of humanity, however, in understanding change and death.

The affirmation should match the tone of the start of the funeral. It can be fairly energetic, an opening salvo against grief, if the life of the deceased was long, full, and positive. It is a good place for a quote, excerpt, or poem. Here are some selections you could use as affirmations:

> *Everyone must leave something behind when he dies, my grandfather said. A child or a book or a painting or a house or a wall built or a pair of shoes made. Or a garden planted. Something your hand touched some way so your soul has somewhere to go when you die, and when people look at that tree or that flower you planted, you're there. It doesn't matter what you do, he said, so as long as you change something from the way it was before you touched it into something that's like you after you take your hands away.* — Ray Bradbury, *Fahrenheit 451*

> *Grief is praise, because it is the natural way love honors what it misses. Grief is centered not in pain but in love.* — Martín Prechtel, *The Smell of Rain on Dust*

*Globed from the atoms falling slow or swift, I see the suns,
I see the systems lift their forms; and even the systems and
the suns shall go back slowly to the eternal drift.* — Lucretius

*Life will break you. Nobody can protect you from that, and
living alone won't either, for solitude will also break you with
its yearning. You have to love. You have to feel. It is the reason
you are here on earth. You are here to risk your heart. You are
here to be swallowed up.* — Louise Erdich, *The Painted Drum*

Using the Humanist manifesto as a guide,[30] I shaped these two simple affirmations:

Life is all. Life is enough. Today we may wish things were different than they are. Still we gather here, sadly but resolutely because we recognize death is a natural part of the challenge of living. As people undaunted by the yet-to-be-known, we draw our full selves up to it.

Life's fulfillment emerges from our participation in the service of humane ideals. We live intending to unfold our fullest possible self and to animate our lives with a deep sense of purpose, finding wonder and awe in the joys and beauties of human existence, its challenges and tragedies, and even in the inevitability and finality of death.

Intention – Give a direct statement about what we are up to today: we are here to acknowledge a death and honor the life lived. It is a little like what you hear at a wedding: "We are gathered here today..." Essentially this is a direct but gentle step validating in a public setting that this death is real. Here are two samples:

We are here because Yvan wanted us to celebrate their life in its fullest, now that they have lived it completely. So although we are sad at their death, we are also here to be thankful and joyful that we knew them.

There's no denying that this day is a sad shock to everyone here. We know Noora wanted more out of life. We know she had many plans and hopes ahead of her. We are going to get through this very difficult day together. We are going to honor Noora's life by remembering how weird and witty and wonderful she was.

As you get more experienced, your welcome, affirmation, and intention will feel less like three separate elements and simply like the natural opening of the ceremony. I spell them out here because when you are new to writing funerals, it can be helpful to deal with them one at a time.

THE MESSAGE ABOUT LIFE AND DEATH - LIFE OUTLOOK OF THE DECEASED

This is the place in the ceremony where we start to make meaning of this event, both in the scope of human culture and in respect to this specific person. In religious ceremonies this would be the sermon. For nonreligious ceremonies it is a blend of your point of view as a celebrant and the point of view and/or values of the deceased and their family. For funerals with a significant eulogy section, this message can simply be a stepping stone to the eulogy(ies). For other funerals, the message might play a greater role.

In religious funerals, this is where you may hear that the deceased is in a better place, is an angel, is waiting to see their family again, is asleep, or will be resurrected. What can a humanist or nonreligious funeral offer that can stand against those hopes? As mentioned previously, I believe we have extra responsibility as nonreligious celebrants to show that this world is as comforting, hopeful, supportive, and compelling as a world in which there is a god or an afterlife. With experience and practice, your messages will round out to be a good mix of the outlook you bring as a nonreligious celebrant with the outlook of the family or the deceased.

EULOGY, TRIBUTE, LIFE PORTRAIT, SOUL SKETCH

An overview of the life of the deceased as told in some thematic way. This critical part of the ceremony is described in greater detail in the chapter on Eulogies.

COMMENDATION

The commendation is a final and formal goodbye to the deceased, spoken as a direct address by the celebrant to the deceased. It acknowledges the life lived and commends them back to the earth, to the realm of memories, or simply to the unknown. For most commendations the celebrant:

- Turns to face the physical remains of the deceased, rather than addressing the mourners
- Speaks to the deceased and uses the second person pronoun "you"
- Is very formal, very brief, just a few sentences
- Includes some sentiment of goodbye or finality

Placing the commendation in the ceremony may be more important than the specific words you say. It is generally placed close to the end of a longer funeral ceremony, possibly just before a final song, the closing words, or the dismissal. In ceremonies with many elements or where you are moving right into a graveside service, you will need to find the right place for it. If a complete funeral is followed immediately by a graveside interment, you might speak the commendation right before the casket is lowered into the ground. Some examples of what to say:

> [*Turn to casket*] "Sivani, you chose a life of science, research, and community. Your desire to know more inspires all those who knew you. We return you now to the greatest unknown, with a sadness made lighter by love."

> "It is time to say farewell to Tina. [*Turn toward urn*] Tina, you were a beloved daughter, sister, aunt, friend, and leader. You were always yourself. We commend you back to the earth, and to our memories forever."

> "We have come to the time today when we must say goodbye to Zenna's body. [*Turn to crematorium retort*] Zenna, you live now in our memories. As you say goodbye to Zenna in your hearts, I will read a poem …"

A commendation can occur in the comprehensive funeral ceremony, in the committal service, or in both. If there will be both a funeral ceremony and a committal service, one way to give yourself more "material" is to have the first commendation acknowledge the characteristics of the deceased, while the second commendation at the committal can be more focused on commending the physical body now received by the earth, fire, etc.

Note that there is confusion and overlap between the terms commendation and committal because not every funeral service you perform will include a physical committal where the body is lowered into the ground or slides into the crematory retort. In those cases, the commendation is used as a sort of "verbal committal" to punctuate the funeral service and give the mourners a sense of finality and farewell. If the family has chosen not to be present at a physical committal, I believe a commendation should be clear and quite distinct as an element during the ceremony.

Both the commendation and the committal are elements inherited from Anglican and Catholic funeral rites, when the dead were committed back to the arms of a god or to heaven. They are not mandatory, but over time secular versions have arisen because they play a useful role: they allow the celebrant to be the one who says, "This is it, this is the final moment, this part of life with your loved one is over, it is time to walk away." Most mourners would find it hard to voluntarily choose a moment of goodbye.

CLOSING WORDS, INVOCATION, WISHES, BENEDICTION, DISMISSAL

Thank again anyone who needs to be thanked. Acknowledge what the family has done, orient them toward living the best values of the deceased, and let people know what to do next. This is the place to add another brief, final message about the life of the deceased, humanist values, and/or what we hold dear that will support the family in the coming weeks, months, and years.

You can also confirm plainly what those gathered have done here. "Today you've done the very difficult thing of caring for Joycee to the very end." You can add an exhortation to live up to the best characteristics of the deceased. "Go and be funny still, be funny again. Joycee's sense of humor is in you and lives on each time you jump out of a closet at someone."

It is wise to have a few phrases at hand that explicitly dismiss the mourners. People often do not know it is ok to leave when the ceremony is formally over. It is a difficult moment for family members, too, if they are essentially leaving their loved one behind in a permanent way. Your role here is to be explicit that the service is over to minimize any social awkwardness they have about doing the right thing.

Writing and Delivering Eulogies

"Am I going to die?"
"Of course you are, it's a matter of time. That's not the right question. Question is: are they going to tell good stories about you when you're gone?"

— The Peanut Butter Falcon

WHAT DID LIFE MEAN TO THIS PERSON? WHAT DID THIS PERSON MEAN TO LIFE?

Eulogies allow us to bring into focus a wholly realized view of the person we loved. It allows mourners to confront both the specificity of the person who has died, and the universality of their values and characteristics. The specificity helps people deal with the present (death, loss); the universality helps people look toward the future (seeing those traits in others, carrying memories forward).

It also shows families aspects or areas of this person's life they might not have known or experienced. That means that eulogies can describe events as disconcerting as learning your mother had another child you were unaware of, and as positive as hearing about how your son, generally argumentative at home, tended to protect bullied children at school. These points of view, from different vantage points, create a fuller picture of the deceased than the one we alone have.

GENERAL GUIDELINES

Aim for a eulogy that is between five and ten minutes long if given by one person - This is between about 750-1600 words. Eulogies by a professional celebrant tend to be more comprehensive and toward the ten-minute mark. The longer the eulogy is, the more dynamic it needs to be to hold the attention of the guests. Short eulogies can be less sophisticated or can touch on a single emotional tone. It is also possible to deliver the eulogy in two main parts, as bookends, and separate them by something like a slideshow, song, or ritual that complements the material in the eulogy.

Share a draft of the eulogy with the NoK as soon as possible or an outline for who is doing what part, how long, and in what order. If I am delivering the eulogy, I like to record an audio file to share with the NoK. Some celebrants read it over the phone. You can send it by email or meet to talk about it. If sending an email, it is a kindness when your subject line clearly states what it is so it can be read in private. Or you can call to let them know you are about to send it. To help people give you good feedback, ask them at least the following three questions:

- Did I get the facts and pronunciations correct?
- Does it include anything sensitive or redundant they would like removed?
- Does it capture the personality of the deceased?

If the eulogy will be delivered among friends and family of the deceased, *aim for a total of about twenty minutes.* You can minimize other aspects of the ceremony if these tributes will be most meaningful to the family. Four to six speakers might speak for five minutes each. You can ask outright if there are people who want to participate in a shared eulogy. Many people value this role and the chance it gives them to honor their loved one. If you end up with a situation where there is a lot of speaking, try to break it up with other elements such as music or a slideshow.

If there are a number of people contributing to the overall eulogy, you have a couple of options to proactively shape this portion of the ceremony. You can engage early with eulogizers and give them direction about what to focus on. This is ideal when there are three or more people, or a wide range of ages or relations.

If there is a variety of speakers and you cannot coordinate with them ahead of time, try at least to get all the stories and speeches in hand prior to the service and impose a form onto them by ordering who speaks first and last, the two positions of greatest emotional impact.

Frequently there are changes on the day of the ceremony. Two grandchildren will decide they want to speak. Someone else forgot their written remarks. Someone brought their guitar and hoped to honor the deceased with their favorite song. If at all possible, try to get written remarks shared with you digitally before the ceremony. In terms of making sure the NoK is aware of and ok with the changes, it is often a good idea to get consent ahead of time by asking, "How would you like me to handle people who ask during the ceremony if they can speak or sing? Is there anyone you would like to prevent from participating?"

If changes to the eulogy or speakers mean big changes to the length of the ceremony, try to check in with the FD during the ceremony to let them know. There is a chance it will change the length of the service and the FD will want to have staff ready at the right time. Occasionally, adding elements will mean an extra cost and they will have information about whether that has been approved by the NoK or not. Also, the FD may have to notify the grounds crew differently if the length of the service is changed.

Eulogy vs. planned remembrances - Eulogies should be treated as fulfilling a specific need and role in the ceremony. Planned remembrances can be shared by people less close, or talking about less central themes, as a way to let people be involved or hear about other aspects of the life of the deceased.

Use humor strategically - Humor may be appropriate for some people and circumstances, and not at all appropriate for others. It should never be mean-spirited or at the expense of the deceased or the bereaved. But it can be self-deprecating or honest about shortcomings. This is another element you can run by the NoK for approval, sharing what you plan to say and asking if you have understood the ceremony's tone correctly.

TYPES OF EULOGIES

The format of eulogies is beginning to open up greatly, from a chronological, culminating list of the deceased's life steps and milestones, to something more like a short story told any number of ways. Not everyone's life is best characterized from being told as a kind of resume or timeline. Actually, almost no one's portrayal benefits from that approach. And chronological eulogies suffer from being written badly and delivered blandly ("...and then Manikka went to Lacita Valley High school, where she was on the golf team and debate team. And then she received her doctorate from UCLA, which she loved attending, and then she opened her practice. It was then that she met.....”). Be open to trying new formats.

Above all, the eulogy is an oral story that should keep the attention and emotional interest of this captive audience. It should be engaging, compelling, dynamic in terms of emotion and delivery, and recognizable as only the deceased was to the people in front of you.

Types of eulogies you can consider include but are not limited to: **chronological, personality traits, life themes, roles, life phases, accomplishments**, and **values**. You will need to gauge from the family how much material there is, how long you have to speak, and who else may be covering parts of the eulogy with their speeches, performances, etc. Sometimes with less "resume" type information, it is good to create a eulogy focused on values or a personality trait.

Chronological

For chronological eulogies, you talk about the life of the deceased "in order" as it happened and ideally bring in universal themes and values as you do so. If a eulogy must be chronological and there are family and friends who would like to deliver parts, it can feel satisfying if one person focuses their eulogy on a particular age or phase of life of the deceased. For instance, a woman in her eighties might be eulogized first by a sibling who talks about her life and interests growing up; then by a spouse who talks about her adult years, ambitions, challenges and compromises; by a son or daughter who talks about her years parenting and the values she passed down; by a grandchild who talks about her role as a grandparent; and finally by a best friend who talks about the vitality, selflessness, and adventure of her later years.

This ensures that the stories are specific, personal, and not an endless listing of facts, even though they are describing the deceased in chronological order. If you are delivering a chronological eulogy, you can also do it by interviewing these people, or asking them to send you memorable vignettes that highlight the personality of the deceased, so you can write and deliver something similar.

Personality Traits and Life Themes

If you were to create a word cloud of all the terms people used to tell you about the deceased, you would end up with something like "personality traits." If, when telling you about the deceased, people use abstract nouns to describe them (adventurous, kind, witty, patient), always ask for specific examples and stories of why. If instead, people are telling you specific stories, see if you can elicit the personality trait. Ask them if you understand correctly. You might hear a story about the deceased running to catch an overnight train in Italy and think it is about their sense of adventure, but it is actually about how frugal they were! But in general, the idea of taking the general and getting specific, or taking specifics and elevating it to something more general, will get you a decent list of characteristics, themes, and anecdotes. As an example, watch Sara Thompson's eulogy of her mother,[31] about three minutes long

If you find a trait that really deserves more attention or time, either because it is significant, or because you need more information to balance out the ceremony, you can ask for more examples of that particular trait. You can also come from around the side, so to speak, and ask family or friends about times when the deceased went against their typical nature.

Flaws, Challenges, Peeves, Learnings, Transformations, and Struggles

Be sure to ask about these aspects of the deceased and their life. They often illustrate important values, relationships, and events that might not look like milestones from the outside, but had an outsized impact on life. If there are enough of these, you can begin to get a sense of a theme that might work for either the eulogy itself or the overall ceremony.

Be careful to not focus on flaws and challenges for people who might not have been well liked. It is ok, for instance, to mention someone being prone to anger, and the ways that affected their outlook on life. It is not ok to give a laundry list of flaws because the family tells them to you in the midst of unrealized anger themselves. Flaws, challenges, and struggles are meant to humanize and specify the person you are eulogizing, not demonize them.

Relationships and Roles

Ask about the major roles the deceased played in their life. You can learn much by seeing who they were in relation to others. After surveying these, look for the common elements, the aspirations, the connections, and the ways the deceased matured or not in various roles. Just one person might encompass all these roles, for example: adoptee, son, middle child, brother, class clown, best friend, car mechanic, boyfriend, veteran, business owner, open adoption advocate, husband, motorcycle enthusiast, uncle, father, business partner, detectorist club leader, driving instructor, grandfather, retiree, and motorcycle mechanic.

Life Phases/States of Being

Rather than focus on specific accomplishments or milestones, you can also consider whether the life of the deceased lends itself to three or four main phases you can talk about. If they are well known by the attendees, this can be a way to view their life "afresh" rather than repeating events that everyone there already knows. For example, you could divide a writer's life into three parts: their nerdy childhood and student experiences; their career as a sci-fi writer; and their intrepid world traveling. Steve Jobs's sister eulogized him by talking about states of being: his full life, his illness, and his dying.[32]

Accomplishments and Regrets

This is similar to the chronological approach, because for many people time corresponds to achievements. However, not everyone takes that approach to life, nor does everyone hop on the Life Elevator and keep going in the same direction. If you can crystallize a few accomplishments—ones that are close to the heart even if they are not anyone else's definition of success—you will have done a good job. In talking about regrets, you can also illustrate what was important to the deceased, even if they fell short. An example might be an older woman who regretted not taking a job as a veterinarian in Rome that she was offered upon graduation, but who fed rock doves on the roof of her building for twenty-five years, took the hurt ones to the vet, and paid for it herself. These actions highlight a unique life and set of values.

Values and Passions

A way to work with specific stories or a lack of detail about someone's life is to talk more about what drove them and their choices in life, and what that tells us about them. Ask yourself what we can learn from what they valued and what they felt compelled to do. One way to ask about this is to ask the family to name the top five things the deceased did with their time. Think about the ways you spend your own time. If the activities themselves are not what you would put in your own eulogy, what instead are the values behind why you do them? What can you learn from those about what is important?

HOW TO WRITE A EULOGY

Ensure you have a list of the major chronological life events of the deceased. Even if you do not write a chronological eulogy, it will help you arrange themes and events in the eulogy you do write. Whether or not the eulogy is delivered as a chronology, documenting the important milestones and punctuations of a person's life is also a good way for you to get oriented and figure out if you need to ask more questions and gather more information and stories.

Review the stories the family shared with you. Determine the themes that emerge from each one. Are the themes of all the stories similar, or is there a lot of variety? If there is significant agreement, you can confidently work those prevailing themes into a eulogy. If there is wild variety, then either the variety itself becomes a theme, or you can turn to another way of organizing the eulogy. This could be anything from an overarching message about how adventurous the deceased was, to a specific moment when the deceased lost a business and it changed the trajectory of the rest of their life.

Before I begin writing the eulogy, I like to have a clear beginning message, usually specific about the deceased, and a clear closing message, usually thematic. That is, I like to know where I am starting and where I am ending up. Not everyone works that way. You may have better success sitting down and simply starting, with the impression of the deceased in mind, to see where it leads you. Regardless of your method, remember that people at a funeral are not hoping for a list of facts or a group of unrelated stories. They are there for a coherent emotional experience. A eulogy with an intentional beginning, middle, and end is one of the most visceral ways to shape that experience.

One way I jump-start my writing is to identify a beloved activity or role the deceased was known for and to use that as connection to the universal values of the deceased. Some examples are a photographer (to illustrate how someone was attentive and creative in his role as a father); tea drinker (for someone who loved England and was a professor of literature); dirt bike rider (someone who kept her family on their toes); mechanic (someone who valued simplicity); and dog walker (someone committed to helping animals and connecting with nature). This approach often provides an easy start that gets you rolling. It also reassures the family that you really got to know their loved one.

Finally, one of the best tips for writing any person's story is to start in the middle. Pick the most dramatic moment of their life. Pick the most uncomfortable moment of their life. Pick the best moment, the most disappointing moment, the transforming moment and *open cold there*. What if instead of avoiding the most embarrassing and painful memory of a person's life, you opened with it? For example:

> It's obvious that James's accident in the '87 Honda back when he was 34 was not his shining moment. The car was totaled. The crates of oranges in the back were juiced well before the

original plan. And his beloved dog, Snout, was killed. By any reckoning it was a disaster. But the accident changed him for the better. A man who had a decade of bad decisions in his rear-view mirror suddenly realized that having fun and being safe were no longer mutually exclusive. His next 18 years were a marvel.

Also, draw in family, friends, and attendees. They are the supporting cast in the stories you are telling, and they are sitting right there. Using the same example:

It's obvious that James's accident in the '87 Honda back when he was 34 was not his shining moment. The car was totaled. The crates of oranges in the back were juiced well before the original plan. And his beloved dog, Snout, was killed. By any reckoning, it was a disaster. **I know some of you are nodding to yourselves. But you're here today because those of you who knew** James before and after the accident know that it changed him for the better. James had a decade of bad decisions in his rear-view mirror. **Many of you felt the impact of those decisions**, good and bad. But after the accident James was a man who realized having fun and being safe were no longer mutually exclusive. His next 18 years were a marvel.

HOW TO DELIVER THE EULOGY

Once you have your written eulogy, you *must* practice reading it aloud. The written voice is very different from the spoken voice and you will always find words that are not the ones you would actually speak, sentence structures that are awkward aloud, and enunciation you need to improve.

Print out a copy and read it aloud at least twice. Mark up that copy with any changes to be made. Rinse and repeat until you are satisfied that you have the wording set. It does not need to be memorized, but this practice is also good preparation for delivering the eulogy with some pauses, glances at the family, smiles at those in the back of the room. You want a eulogy that is warm, approachable, and somewhat dynamic in its tone. Something with cadence, variety, and emotional range.

Once you have the final written version, you should now practice for pace and dynamics. As you speak, imagine that you are speaking to a very receptive and forgiving crowd. Generally, the attendees at a funeral will be both of those things. They will usually notice the specifics of the eulogy during the funeral, but what tends to last in their memories is the tone and emotional connection.

The nearest analogy I can give for the "how" of delivering the eulogy is: like a good bedtime story. The story needs to lead the listeners into it, but it is ok if the details evade memory later. Its job is just as much to create a feeling as to deliver facts.

You can make helpful notes on your hard copy. For example, I CAPITALIZE words I need to say more clearly or slowly. I underline words I want to accent. Sometimes I even give myself [BIG SMILE] stage directions.

A pleasant speaking pace for this part of a funeral is somewhere between 155-165 words per minute. You can find this pace by reading a more formally written passage for one minute. There are some practice readings included in this book so you can time yourself and develop a good speaking voice. Read a passage aloud three times and average your speaking time. During the funeral service, it is completely normal to pause for longer than you might usually. You can grab a moment for an emotional break, take a sip of water, or just gather your thoughts as you arrive at the more important, somber, or dramatic parts of the eulogy.

Regarding technology for your spoken matter and the eulogy, figure out if you're comfortable with only digital, or a digital and paper backup, or solely paper. Personally, I always have a paper backup copy. Botching this important moment due to batteries dying or a poor internet connection is unprofessional. More and more often I use an e-reader, and have the paper copy so I can shift easily if something happens and the e-reader does not work.

Committal Services

Also known as a graveside service, interment, final disposition, or simply the committal

One of the reasons we feel so strongly about having a body present for a funeral is to allow the bereaved to make a final physical goodbye. The committal is the threshold moment in a funeral. It is when the body is transformed from one state into another, or is being received into its final resting place. It is when the casket moves into the crematory retort at a witnessed cremation. It is when the casket is lowered during a graveside service. It is when the ashes are scattered. It is when the urn is placed in the niche. It might even be when the Next of Kin receives back ashes made into jewelry. It is usually the most emotional and formal moment of the service.

You will encounter and conduct committals in a few different forms. If there is a funeral ceremony and then the mourners go to the cemetery for a graveside service for the casket to be buried, that graveside service is the committal. If the family is witnessing the cremation before, after, or instead of a more ceremonial funeral, that is a committal. If family and friends have not had any ceremony and they want to have an ash scattering, that is a committal.

In terms of trends, in my area there seems to be a move away from having a large funeral ceremony followed by a committal of some sort, and toward having a direct cremation or direct burial and then a graveside service (aka, a committal) as the only funeral ceremony. When a committal follows a complete funeral ceremony, the committal is usually very brief. If the committal is the only service, though, the family may envision it as a hybrid between a complete funeral and a committal. Most families don't know these terms or see much distinction between them. They only know they want to mark the death of a loved one and have chosen this threshold moment for it. You will have to probe to understand what the family has in mind.

On the flip side, not every family wants to be present for a committal. You may conduct funeral ceremonies that end at the funeral home and no one goes on to the cemetery for a burial. Or no one witnesses the cremation. However, I favor families witnessing the physical committal for two reasons. One is that it helps the family literally know where their loved one is. I think there is a realism and a self-kindness in knowing that. The other is that it helps move the family along the bumpy road of grief, because it encourages them to take the active step of leaving the deceased behind physically. You can let them know that many people find it transformational to be present for that moment of separation. But in the end, it is their choice.

If you will be offering committal services here are some guidelines:

- Aim for a committal that is about ten minutes long if there has already been a comprehensive funeral. If the committal/ graveside funeral/witnessed cremation is the only ceremony, it can be longer but generally not more than thirty minutes in my experience. Some of that will depend on the weather, setup, and abilities of the guests. There may be tents and chairs, or you may be exposed to rain, cold, or heat. Witnessed cremations can flow more seamlessly, and run longer, from a funeral service into the committal portion.
- Committals tend to be conducted by the celebrant with little or no participation from the attendees, and sometimes no speaking participation at all. Sometimes there are spontaneous remembrances, a call-and-response benediction, singing, or a short reading.
- Committals tend to be more serious and to have restrained rituals, if any. The tone is usually formal, wistful, or sweet, though you may encounter families who want joyful committals. In my experience, even the most upbeat family arrives at a serious point during a committal where it is hard to round the corner back to joy, but they can usually make the turn with your help.

- For burial of urns, I feel it is ok for the family to stay for the entire burial. It can be a bit abrupt but the grounds crew (usually one person for an urn) will come, shovel dirt into the hole, rake it over so that the ground does not show a mound, and then they replace the plug of grass that was cut for the whole. For a niche, they close up the panel with some screwdrivers or mallet. It is about ten minutes. For caskets, it is a longer process and often involves a backhoe, which is difficult for families to be confronted with. Usually lowering the casket is enough completion.
- Some families will want to participate in the burial by casting or shoveling dirt. Cemeteries have different policies for what they allow families to do and to stay for, so confirm it in advance before offering the option to the family.
- It is my opinion that you do the family a service by ending the committal clearly and cleanly. You can end the graveside ceremony service decisively and simply by telling the mourners the ceremony is over and it is time to go. This gives them permission to literally turn their back on the deceased, which is very difficult.

Committals and commendations are two different parts of the funeral ceremony that have similar feel and purpose. You may encounter people who use the words interchangeably. Most families will not know or care about the differences. But they are jargon that will help you understand and write the ceremony. For our training, I treat them as separate elements. As your practice grows you will feel more comfortable using the terms in various situations.

Part 3.
Personalizing End-of-Life Ceremonies

Place and Setting

You will not usually be involved in choosing the locations and settings for the end-of-life ceremonies you perform, but based on what you know about the setting, you can make some guesses about the tone, the level of formality, the length of the ceremony, and rituals it will be possible (or impossible) to do. You will have more options, for instance, in a cemetery's non-denominational chapel with ready-room, microphones, music system, and candles than you will at a beach. As always, confirm with the family any assumptions you are making about the setting's influence on the ceremony.

The most common settings are:
- Funeral home
- Cemetery chapel (many different sizes, styles, moods)
- Cemetery cremation chapel or waiting room
- Grave site
- Private venue (rented) such as a restaurant, museum, or event space. These are very common for memorial services but not unheard of for funerals.
- Private home, sometimes the deceased's
- Public or private outdoor location such as a park, riverway, or woods, and usually only for cremated remains

One thing you can control as a celebrant is the settings where you would like to work, such as funeral homes that are convenient to you, cemeteries you think are especially beautiful or important, and venues that would be a good fit for your types of ceremonies. Reach out to see if you can be added to their list of celebrants. If you feel particularly in tune with some settings and what they reflect in terms of beliefs and style, then by all means take steps to be the celebrant they think of first!

Readings

The written word, in the form of poetry, literature, and quotes, is one of the most useful tools for celebrants. For the sake of simplicity, I will refer to these all as readings. Readings can be used to:

- convey the personality of the deceased, either through specific favorites of the deceased, or because you find readings that reflect or amplify what you learn from the family
- complement the emotional needs and meaning-making of the mourners
- intentionally move the ceremony forward with pace, direction, punctuation, or tone
- extend the length of a ceremony that is thin on other material but is not yet the funeral you are trying to deliver
- involve mourners by giving them the role of reader
- elevate and play off of your own writing in the surrounding material
- convey your point of view as a celebrant

Like most ceremony elements, readings work best when incorporated intentionally as part of a harmonious whole. Using seven or eight very short quotes in a ceremony feels different than using a two-page excerpt from a book. There may be ceremonies where one of those is appropriate, but for those readings to feel befitting they should balance whatever else is happening in the ceremony.

Ensure the ceremony tone and readings work together. If the overall tone of the ceremony is a celebration of life but the readings are extremely somber, they will tug the mood downward. If the ceremony is thoroughly sad but the readings are upbeat, they may be irritating at best and emotionally alienating at worst.

Finally, for most end-of-life ceremonies it makes sense to place readings that are somber, formal, or that look to the past toward the beginning of the service. Readings that are more upbeat, casual, and future-focused work best toward the end. Doing this validates the emotions that most mourners arrive with. It helps carry them over the literal threshold of the end of the ceremony and out into a world which has not stopped because their loved one is dead, but which is now very different.

In practice, you will most likely work with specific readings the family tells you they want to include, or readings that you suggest to families from your own library. Here are some things to consider for each situation.

When you work with readings that families request, you will need to read them to assess them first for length, tone, and where it makes sense to include the piece. If someone else will be reading the passage, note on your outline who they are. You should also read the piece to make sure there is nothing you feel uncomfortable reading if it falls to you to read it during the ceremony. Often, I also bring a point of view to readings about whether an author is generally problematic (now known to be overtly racist, misogynist, etc.) or situationally problematic (for instance, a reading from Harry Potter might be inappropriate for the funeral of a trans person).

Some readings may also tip toward cultural appropriation versus cultural appreciation. For example, you may be hired to perform the service for someone who was very proud to be a Mayflower descendant. If their family wants to incorporate a reading from a Native American tribe leader, it might be appropriation. In the same way that a priest, rabbi, or imam would not parrot the words of another religion without some discernment, you as a nonreligious celebrant can help protect the integrity of cultures that are marginalized, colonized, or oppressed.

Another thing you can do is make an effort to attribute all readings, at least in any printed matter. Historically people have attributed quotes and readings by prominent authors, and have ignored attributing works by women, people of color, native peoples, or others not deemed important by the norms of the time. Attribution is one way to make sure your ceremonies are genuinely inclusive and that all authors are recognized.

When searching for a reading to suggest to families, here are a few guiding thoughts to help you narrow the choices: First, is there a place in the ceremony that needs some content? If so, what is the right length, tone, and/or message for that place in the ceremony? Second, what are the broad themes and messages of the life of the deceased? Based on those, what can you find to reflect those?

In terms of sharing ideas with families, I find it easiest to first suggest specific readings by pasting the reading into an email or attaching a doc. If the family does not like any of the initial suggestions, then I share my entire collection of readings with them so they can read more on their own.

RIFFING ON RELIGIOUS READINGS

Religious prayer can be moving and effective because it reaches the level of ritual: it is formal, it is a shared experience, it is physical, and it connects people to universal themes. It is possible to emulate the experience of prayer as a humanist without invoking a god by using some of the same structures, pacing, and scope of prayer language. Keep this in mind if you are working with a family who wants a nonreligious service but have a soft spot for formal elements or that element of nostalgia they remember from church, mosque, or synagogue.

As an example, for a grief ceremony I created, I wanted a place in the ceremony for a formal entreaty that reminds participants of our connection to something we are a part of, but dwarfed by. Because I grew up Catholic, the structure of the Lord's Prayer echoed in my history. I did some research on the prayer, then tried to match its structure while focusing on humanist values.

Music

Music at its best...is the grand archeology into and transfiguration of our guttural cry, the great human effort to grasp in time our deepest passions and yearnings as prisoners of time. Profound music leads us—beyond language—to the dark roots of our scream and the celestial heights of our silence.

— Cornel West, *The Cornel West Reader*

Music is one of the easiest and most accessible tools in the toolkit for funeral celebrants. You can learn a lot about a person by asking about their music preferences and tastes. It often reveals a generational sense of belonging, a personal relationship to culture, their creative impulse, and their unique point of view. So, by all means, ask about the deceased's taste in music and be supportive of ways to include it in the funeral.

Music also announces the tone of the funeral in no uncertain way. When a funeral ceremony you attend opens with Bill Withers' *Ain't No Sunshine*[33] you will sense it is one kind of service. When it starts with Pentatonix's *Sound of Silence*,[34] *Orfeo Ed Euridice* by The Berlin Symphonic Orchestra,[35] or Barbra Streisand's *Don't Rain on My Parade*,[36] you will sense it is another. The music that closes the ceremony will also greatly affect the outgoing mood of the mourners.

There are many other ways and places to use music—and more generally, soundscape—in the service. Music and sound, more than almost any other element of the ceremony, will take whatever emotions are floating out loose among the mourners and organize them, give them some coherence. Therefore, use music primarily to validate a shared emotion or gently shepherd people toward a new one. Do not use it to manipulate emotions—for instance, to end the ceremony on a more upbeat emotion than mourners will be able to attain. But you can choose music that starts where mourners are emotionally and encourages them in a specific direction, just like a DJ who matches the current mood and brings you to another one.

Who chooses the music? Generally you can ask the NoK to tell you about the musical tastes of the deceased and any of their own wishes for music. Sometimes there is already a sense that someone will want to perform a piece live. If that is the case, try to listen in advance to pieces people want to sing or play (via YouTube or a music streaming service) so you have a better idea of where to place them in the ceremony. You can also ask the musicians to send you a rough copy digitally so you have a sense of their rendition and how long it will be. This can be helpful to have in your "back pocket." If there are technical issues with live versions, it might be possible to play their recorded version.

More somber, wistful solos or acapella songs generally fit well at the beginnings of a ceremony. Perhaps even before your welcome and opening words. More upbeat, amplified, or instrumental pieces often fit better toward the end or as the close. But sometimes you will simply need to place them to achieve some variety in the ceremony. If there is a lot of music, you can layer some sounds with other elements. Depending on the actual song and style, they can work well behind a slideshow, as accompaniment to a ritual, or as soft background to moments of silent introspection.

When there is no live music by friends and family, the responsibility for suggesting some specific music (or soundscapes) may be yours. Many celebrants make YouTube playlists to share with families to listen to suggested songs. If you have a music streaming service, you can create them there, too. Often I will listen to other people's funeral playlists and save the songs I think my type of family would find appropriate.

Also remember that these days you can expand from actual songs into soundscapes, especially for nature lovers. You could close a ceremony for someone who loved birding with birdsong; open for a surfer with ocean waves; have a moment of reflection for a kayaker with the sound of oars.

If you are not a music person, you can seek out suggested lists and sift those for what you feel is most in keeping with the ceremonies you envision creating. Remember that the music you suggest can say as much about you and your life stance as the music the family asks for says about the deceased. So, if you have a musical point of view for funeral ceremonies, do not be afraid to explore it. On the other hand, it is also ok to let families know you do not handle music suggestions, but only where to place them in the ceremony. If you are supporting them in most of the other ceremonial ways, it is ok to have an area that you are simply not the right person for.

In terms of the technical needs for playing music during funerals, most but not all funeral homes, cemeteries, and crematoria have ways of playing music. When you learn what the venue is, it is best to check in about technology and electrical capabilities and constraints. Ask if they are open to having live music played, what the electrical setup is, whether there is a house sound system (PA, amplifiers, etc.), or whether musicians need to bring their own, how early they can set up, whether there is a house device and music streaming service (like a tablet and Spotify, for example) that you will be able to use, and how you will get songs on it. If you have not conducted a service at the location before, also get a sense of how big the space is. A brass band might overwhelm a living room-sized space at a funeral home and you could suggest they play outside when the casket is moved. A soloist singer might get lost sonically at a graveside service outdoors near heavy traffic.

More specific to sound logistics, I recommend not using your own phone for providing sound unless it is dedicated to that specific job. It is too easy for ads to come up during YouTube playlists and streaming services, too easy for phone calls to accidentally ring through, or notifications to interrupt. As a celebrant it is one less thing to worry about if you use the funeral home's or Next of Kin's device.

For all multimedia aspects of ceremonies, when the ceremony happens quickly after death, there is often not time for you to accomplish all of this personally because you are focused on writing. As your ceremonies get easier to put together, you may have more bandwidth for other kinds of support like providing music or creating slideshows.

Rituals

Rituals are meant to help us navigate unfamiliar and extraordinary events by giving shape to emotions and by acting as "containers" for emotional states. This is especially true around the end of life because most primary mourners are experiencing high levels of distress, significant unfamiliarity, and intense scrutiny from the community, whether it be questions about how they are holding up, to guesses about a cause of death, to judgment about the funeral elements.

Rituals also give us a way to make abstract, symbolic notions like *love* or *community* perceptible in time and space. They are a gesture against the immensity of time and space to say, "Our sibling Merritt was here. They existed and were seen. They had a time and a place." Some rituals that do this include placing headstones, signing a guestbook, casting dirt from the hometown of the deceased into the burial site, showing photos of the deceased, and telling stories (tributes, remembrances) about them.

Rituals proclaim that the positive characteristics of our loved one continue on, that we will keep their memory alive, that something about them is timeless. Some rituals that do this include gestures with living objects, breathing, movement, or beginnings. Common examples of this are lush flowers surrounding an urn or photo of the deceased, lighting candles, singing, or releasing doves.

Funeral rituals invite us to admit death, impermanence, and loss. Traditional rituals that do this include extinguishing candles, casting dirt into the burial site, casting petals onto the burial vessel, putting things "away" like folding the flag, releasing doves, and formally turning our backs to the deceased.

Rituals can also bring in personal meaning and connection to history and ancestry when the deceased or their family has cultural, ethnic, or religious traditions they want to honor.

Rituals can invoke formal beauty by incorporating shapes, especially the shapes we gather in. Circles, semi-circles, straight lines, and repetition or multiples have a particular impact on our emotional state. Picture the shapes of a drumming circle, the formation of a receiving line, or mandalas made from a material unique to the deceased (embroidery thread, shot glasses, origami).

One of the most important purposes of rituals in end-of-life ceremonies is to keep those gathered connected to their bodies. People who are grieving describe feelings of floating apart from life, a sense of unreality, feeling hollow, disconnected. Many struggle with basic care such as eating and sleeping. Rituals and gestures can be ways a community helps itself stay present and embodied. Asking mourners to light a candle, to sing, to fold the flag—these are all ways we help them literally move through mourning practices.

GENERAL GUIDELINES

Rituals for end-of-life ceremonies fall into two large categories: **formal** (or structural), and **personal**. Formal rituals announce that we are at a ceremony, that we are doing something special, that it is time to shift our presence. Using the example of a wedding, the phrase *Dearly beloved* does this. It has nothing to do with the personality of the couple and everything to do with signaling that this time and space is special.

Personal rituals, on the other hand, represent the unique characteristics of the person being honored. They reinforce for the grieving that they cherished the bundle of accomplishments, quirks, regrets, loves, peeves, and values of a specific person.

As a general rule, I use formal rituals to open and close the ceremony. They are deeply reassuring to the primary mourners. Anything that begins will end. As difficult as a funeral is, once begun it too will end. For families, the end-of-life service lets them know they are almost done with one of the hardest things. Ending the funeral clearly is also important, because the end is a relief to mourners. They can tell themselves, "We got through that," "We did the right thing," "We really honored them well." In the absence of a clear ending, families are left wondering what is next or if they have done it right.

Personal rituals feel more natural in the main part of the ceremony, or when interacting with any remains or with the attendees. These usually become clear as you are talking with the family or getting to know the deceased. Someone's love of basketball will give you an idea for people to stand in a free throw formation around the casket at the gravesite. Someone's knitting hobby will give you the idea to wrap yarn around the urn before it's buried.

But these are not rules set in stone. Be ready and willing to make a ritual fit the situation. A formal opening ritual to signal the start of the funeral can be transformed into a personal gesture. If someone was in a band, one of the family members could start the ceremony with a crash of cymbals, a drum roll, or a guitar lick from their favorite song. And if it fits the person or the tone, a somewhat formal ritual during the eulogy or remembrance might work. Sometimes there is overlap between formal and personal. A man who insisted on having lit candles on the table for every dinner with his grandchildren might have a funeral that begins with all his grandchildren lighting a mass of candles. When appropriate, using both kinds of rituals in your ceremony can be most satisfying and effective for mourners.

When the deceased or their family wants to update a cultural, ethnic, or religious tradition, it is often helpful to ask the family what is most important for them about the ritual, and then possibly to research the tradition so you can think about ways to revise it into a more universal ritual.

WHEN AND HOW TO USE RITUAL IN FUNERALS

The first bit of advice is not to overcomplicate funerals. The overall feel of the day lasts much longer than specific actions and rituals. Second, placing rituals in an end-of-life ceremony is a little different. There are two main "honorees" of the ceremony: one is the deceased and the other is the family/friends gathered. Each goes through a different transformation.

In terms of the deceased, the ceremony gently symbolizes the change in this person's state from alive to dead. We begin with elements that suggest life and, as the service progresses, those rituals and elements become more static or lifeless. So the most personal and "alive" elements should be placed toward the beginning of the ceremony. Examples of this are lighting a candle, surrounding the urn with live flowers, raising something up, bringing things together, opening something, using video images, brightly colored photos, etc.

As the ceremony continues and closes, rituals involving the deceased then use elements or gestures that symbolize death and endings, such as dirt, loose petals, scattering, closing, covering, extinguishing, watching something recede, using a still image in black and white, etc. A classic formal example is to start with the casket open, and to end by closing it. A very personal example is placing a favorite tea cup on the table with the ashes. At the beginning of the ceremony the partner of the deceased fills the cup. At the end, they drink it or pour it out.

Conversely, in terms of the actions and emotions of the family and guests it seems to go best when their rituals and gestures move from death to life, from looking back to looking forward. For instance, music that opens the ceremony might be somber but music that closes the ceremony might be upbeat; readings at the beginning of the ceremony can be focused on loss, distance, and sadness, and readings toward the end might focus more on a future made peaceful through community support, memories, etc.; guests may arrive and place small stones on the ground near an urn symbolizing inanimate permanence, and as they leave they might be given the favorite recipe of the deceased to symbolize nourishment. The emotional path you are laying for them is from shock and confrontation of death, to turning again toward life and creation. Elements that connect the bereaved to the universal may feel more natural coming at the end of a ceremony, as they help mourners leave knowing that this life meant something.

HUMANIST RITUALS

Personal rituals are best discovered and created in conversation with family, but you can generate ideas for rituals from humanist themes like nature, science, art, literature, relationships, personality, and emotion. My opinion about religious rituals, in fact, is that they are based on the same basic ingredients as all rituals (such as time, fire, water, earth, air, and the five senses), and that they likely came before religion. One way to rework religious rituals for nonreligious ceremonies is to incorporate the same elements in a different way. Using an ornate Catholic-style incense holder to waft frankincense and myrrh would not be appropriate for a humanist funeral, but placing piñon incense around the casket could be.

When thinking about nonreligious rituals, you can use these possible ingredients below to spur your creativity and imagination.

Nature and Science
- Flowers and flora native to an area special to the deceased, or because they especially liked them
- Rocks brought by attendees to pile near an urn or on a table with a photo of the deceased
- A bowl of water where guests wash hands on arrival
- A soundscape of birdsong that gradually increases volume to open the ceremony
- Invoking the seasons through color or natural elements
- Garlands and repetition of natural objects, like a mandala of acorns or fall leaves
- Noting the large-scale or astronomical moments of the time of birth, time of death, time of burial, like the position of the sun, sunrise, season, angle of the earth, sunset, moonrise, prominent stars
- Using maps of special areas for a traveler
- Invoking creatures that reflect the personality or characteristics of the deceased, especially if they were explicit about this relationship (a cat person, a beekeeper, a "lone wolf," a "social butterfly")

Art and Literature
- Quotes from literature or lyrics turned into a bookmark
- Colors from a favorite piece of artwork, worked into the setting or ceremony
- Quotes from artists about the meaning of life, the value of art, the point of beauty, hope
- A stack of favorite books on the table with a guestbook
- Riffing on a meaningful word in multiple languages for someone who was multilingual
- Making a set of pennants with kind words about the deceased
- Signing quilt squares that someone will make into a quilt

Relationships and Personality
- Quotes from family and friends about the deceased
- A "word cloud" made of attributes and comments about the deceased
- Artifacts that represent each role the person had
- Elements from their own personal rituals (tea, dog-walking, reading aloud to grandchildren)
- Things they used in their hobbies (fishing, sewing, kites, music)

The Senses
- Hearing: Background music or soundscape, opening chime or an attention-getting sound, call and response, singing, live or recorded music, clapping
- Smell: Flowers or live natural elements, pine boughs, candles, essential oils, incense, a signature perfume or cologne, baked goods, herbs, tea
- Sight: Photos, collages, videos, artwork
- Touch: Iconic clothing the deceased wore, a quilt, receiving lines, hugs, small stones to "worry" during the service
- Taste: This sense is often met by a reception or meal after the funeral, but you can also include favorite foods into the ceremony, like having boxes of Red Hots or Junior Mints for a candy lover, etc. or giving out a recipe to everyone who attends
- Movement: Re-enacting ritual movements that were important to the deceased like a tea ceremony, walking, martial arts

forms, or dance, as well as funeral-specific motions like
carrying the casket, walking behind the casket, shoveling dirt

RITUAL STRUCTURE

Once you have ideas for ingredients, now you need to structure
the materials into a form that elevates the experience to a ritual.
I find that mixing and matching elements, physical senses, and
patterns almost always results in something with meaning,
symbolism, and personality.

Elements	Senses	Shapes & Patterns
Water Air Earth Fire	See (color, light) Hear Smell Touch Taste Coordinated movements	Circle, triangle, square, others Half circle, arc, arch, spiral Straight lines Repetition, multiples

For example, a ritual that joins air and the sense of sound and
repetition might be as simple as asking all guests to face west and
listen to the sounds of the wind against the trees before scattering
some ashes. Or it might be a drum corps arranged in a line (more
formal) or a circle (more informal). A ritual that joins water and
taste might be a toast to the deceased, or pouring out a favorite
drink on the grave site. For a remarkable example of sound plus
movement plus multiples, watch the funeral haka for New Zealand
rugby star Jonah Lomu.[37] It is an extraordinary funeral ceremony
for a public figure full of ritual and symbolic elements.

For gestures that depend on technology or on custom elements,
it is ok to have the family be responsible for supplying the
materials. It is a lot to create the ceremony itself in a short time
frame and also be responsible for the materials. As you gain more
experience, you will feel confident about taking on additional roles.
You might look into a few local printers, florists, and other vendors
or suppliers before you start conducting funerals. Many funeral
homes also have long-standing vendor connections you can use.

Difficult Ceremonies

Funerals bring with them an enormous variety of circumstances that may impact the emotions and needs of the bereaved. Where weddings usually have at least a veneer of happiness and a dependable set of roles, death has more variables. The age of the deceased, the manner of death, the length of the dying process, the emotional tone of the relationships they had, and the logistical steps to holding the ceremony all play a role. Consider all of these examples of normal deaths:

- a 24-year-old man's drug overdose;
- a solitary woman in her 90s with dementia, of old age;
- a 57-year-old veteran's suicide;
- a newborn's stillbirth in hospital;
- a teen's accidental death in a skiing accident;
- a problematic and disliked patriarch, in his late 80s, of a heart attack;
- a person with only a handful of family or friends who have no real momentum for ceremony; and
- a ceremony held completely online due to pandemic constraints.

The situations of a single death are multifaceted and will not always be shared with you. As a result, you may have to keep your antenna up a bit more than with other ceremonies to determine things like whether the family has much energy for the ceremony or is feeling complicated emotions about the death. One of the benefits of working with a FD is that you can communicate much more directly with them.

As long as you are warm, reassuring, professional, and approachable, there is generally no need to do anything vastly special or different in the cases of difficult deaths. As in all interactions with the family, simply do your best to be a calm presence, a supportive listener, and be open to what matters most to them. What are the most important elements of the ceremony for them? When they think back on this day, what will have made it a bit easier? You can ask the family directly if they want the cause of death mentioned, perhaps in terms of donations, or not mentioned at all. But note that charitable causes do not always align with the cause of death and you almost never need to know it. Alternately, some families may want you to mention it in the ceremony, as with messages about awareness about skin cancer, substance abuse, suicide, drowning, mental health, or SIDS.

One thing you *can* do to prepare for difficult funerals is create a basic funeral ceremony before you are hired for one. In my experience it is much easier to write a ceremony when you have more time, when you can think objectively about different sections and assess readings, and when you are not absorbing strong emotions from the bereaved. Write two opening and closing sections: one that feels appropriate for "neutral" deaths and one for difficult deaths. Identify some readings ahead of time. Then when faced with an actual funeral, you can focus on writing the eulogy and seeding your ceremony with personalized touches.

YOUR OWN EMOTIONS - THE ELEPHANT IN THE ROOM

One variable here is your own emotional state in the face of difficult deaths and ceremonies. After a few funerals you will begin to understand which direction your emotional weather vane tends to turn, and how to account for it. For instance, I tend to experience the opposite emotions as the group of mourners. If they are visibly upset, crying, leaning on each other, sharing stories and anecdotes profusely, I usually find it easy to remain in a wholly professional facilitator role. Whereas for ceremonies where the family is emotionally private or has an active dislike of the deceased, I tend to feel sad, as if some part of me needs to bring some mourning to the event.

Now that I know this, I have a few things I can say or do to smooth over any of my own ripples as they arise in a ceremony. If I get a little choked up, I will pause, breathe. If my emotions rise more noticeably I might say something like, "I'm very moved by your presence here for Sharlette."

You will find celebrants who believe you should never express emotion; others who believe you should of course express emotion. The main point is that the emotional needs of the family are the ones being served and supported during the funeral. Yours, even as you are experiencing them in the moment, need to be kept at the level where no one needs to put their emotions aside to care for yours. You will need to know your emotional neutral zone, and ways to find it while keeping the family's emotions centered. Make a plan for after the ceremony when there is time to take care of yourself through your own rituals.

DEATH BY DRUG OVERDOSE/SUBSTANCE ABUSE

In my experience, deaths involving or from substance abuse can leave families ashamed and sometimes reluctant to have any ceremony at all, but they still want to "do something." If there is very little information coming from the family, generally I turn toward more structural rituals like the opening and closing elements. I ask about music and hobby habits of the deceased, trying to work in even just a line or quote somewhat formally, mentioning that it was something of a favorite of the deceased. If the family is open to it, I leave room for family and guests to share remembrances. Eulogies of the young can sometimes feel like a further reminder of a life cut short. If you feel like you have enough to work with, proceed, but you can also depend simply on remembrances from others, or provide a less personal message for the main part of the ceremony.

One additional thing to be aware of is that families may have a great deal of anger toward any friends or relatives that the deceased used drugs with. This might result in private or very small ceremonies. It might seem to you that the deceased had no friends, when actually it is because the family does not want them there. Having friends of the deceased at the service might also mean difficult interactions between guests. Ask the primary decision-maker if there are interactions they are worried about. Think about ways that rituals or choreography could insulate them from strained interactions. Perhaps the family enters and exits formally without any mingling. Perhaps spontaneous memories are not offered during the ceremony but you make a request to email them. And you can share the information with the FD so they can be aware of the possibility. FDs have experience with calmly but firmly handling conflict at a ceremony.

DEATH BY ALZHEIMER'S/DEMENTIA

As medical advances and interventions lead to longer lives, conditions like Alzheimer's and dementia are more frequent conditions the elderly die with or of. For many of their families, death is a second stage of grief, and sometimes an easier stage than the years living with a parent or spouse with dementia. If someone has been caring for a relative with dementia, it may be hard for them to access memories of the distant past when things were simpler or happier. This is a situation where looking at photos and talking about roles can help bring out a fuller portrayal of the deceased. Many families, and specifically primary caregivers, may have guilt and relief that a very difficult phase of care is over. Be as professionally reassuring as possible. You can assure people that death brings up a lot of feelings at once, and that that's ok.

In addition to funerals for those who had dementia, a fellow funeral celebrant in England has spearheaded ways to create funerals that are dementia-friendly,[38] for when those living with dementia and their caregivers are attending.

DEATH BY SUICIDE

This is another situation when you may encounter shame and anger from various family members or between them. If the family has been open about those emotions, it can be ok to represent some of that during the ceremony. You might say something like, "Suicide can leave a lot of unfinished business and conflicting emotions. Is it ok if I mention that, if I say it aloud? Usually that makes more room to remember Natalie's wonderful qualities."

If you get the ok, ask the family if they want to hear that part beforehand. Placing it early in the ceremony creates a pivot point to sadness and grief. For the ceremony wording you might say, "Yes, there is a lot of anger toward Jordan for ending his life. We feel rejected, powerless, and ashamed. But we know better than anyone, better even than Jordan knew, how much he was loved. How much he made a difference in our lives."

It might be helpful to know that current research on suicide shows it is not good to say that someone *committed* suicide.[39] It has echoes of committing a crime or a sin, rather than seeing suicide as a result of mental health issues or split-second emotional distress. It is also often said someone "successfully" committed suicide after a few "failed attempts" which may lead to an increased view of suicide as something positive, which is a concern in the United States at a time when suicide is a rising cause of death. Even more concerning:

> In 2020, research demonstrated that stigmatizing and other verbiage commonly used in regard to suicide, such as reporting or sharing the method of suicide leads to a 13% increase in the national suicide rate following highly publicized (celebrity) suicides as well as a 30% increase in suicides completed in the same method as the public figure.[40]

Because it has been observed that suicides rates can also rise in groups where a loved one or acquaintance died by suicide,[41, 42] many funeral ceremonies now also provide brochures or announcements about hotlines and mental health support.

What to say instead: died by suicide, ended his life, was experiencing mental illness, took her life.

Similar shifts in language have occurred for "physician-assisted suicide," or "medical suicide" to describe the deliberate ending of one's life with the support of a medical professional. It is available in limited places in the United States, generally to people who have a terminal illness and less than six months to live, and the mental capacity to choose this way to die. Though legal in only nine states and in the District of Columbia, "a 2018 poll by Gallup displayed that a solid majority of Americans—about 72%—support laws allowing patients to seek the assistance of a physician in ending their life."[43]

What to say instead: medical aid in dying, physician-assisted dying, medically-assisted death, chose a death with dignity, or ended his life with dignity.

Keep your ears and mind open among the communities you serve for the things that affect them. Have an active commitment to being open to new ways of doing things.

DEATHS OF CHILDREN

[In] burying children we bury the future, unwieldy and unknown, full of promise and possibilities, outcomes punctuated by our rosy hopes. The grief has no borders, no limits, no known ends, and the little infant graves that edge the corners and fencerows of every cemetery are never quite big enough to contain that grief. Some sadnesses are permanent. Dead babies do not give us memories, they give us dreams.

— Thomas Lynch, *The Undertaking*

Aside from the emotions present in funerals for children, other challenges are easy to understand. Thinking about the main elements of funeral design, services for infants and children mean many choices will be made already. Tone? Usually, but not always, sad, somber, or reflective. Creating meaning for the mourners? That is a difficult task. Encouraging parents, grandparents, and siblings to accept this death may be unrealistic. You might focus on the meaning the baby or child had for the parents or bereaved, rather than the meaning the child was able to make of their own life. Beliefs? Instead of highlighting the beliefs of the deceased, you turn to the beliefs of the closest family members. Their beliefs—religious or not—may be inadequate for this day and situation. Trying to offer your own beliefs can backfire. Do not offer platitudes or clichés. Do not tell them the funeral will make them feel better or help them process the grief.

Stories? With a teen or school-age child there will be stories. Sometimes the stories are the kind that form that bridge from personality to universal qualities, but sometimes they will simply be memories, without the added heft of having yet become personality traits and values. With infants there will be even less to draw on. Symbols and rituals? This is where you may focus most of the ceremony, on the beats that move the family from the start of the day to the end of it, so the one thing they can find solace in is that it is over.

All that said, however, it is important to be guided by the actual emotions of the parents. One infant funeral I conducted was purposely uplifting. The parents genuinely wanted to transform the day into something positive. Some suggestions for how to write a funeral for a child:

- If using an affirmation, tune it to the emotions of the parents. In fact, you might break the "rule" of affirmations and instead use the time to deny instead of affirm. An example I have written: "This is a day no one wants. It's an enormous No. No to the empty crib. No to the empty car seat. No to the empty stroller. No to your empty arms. No to a world without Bellamy. This is a day no one wants."
- For the intention of the gathering, consider posing it as a question: "Why are we here? We arrive here, sitting together, to face this small casket. Why do we do this?" This shift lets your message focus on the shared humanity of funerals in general, rather than trying to write details about a short life.
- Eulogies can focus on what the child meant to their family members, and how they played a role as part of a constellation of joy.
- Affirm the reality of sadness, but do not pile on or be melodramatic. The family's emotions are the ones you need to make room for, not your own.
- Music can be a good element because there are so many songs associated with childhood, and it gives the grieving some focus.
- Keep it short unless a long ceremony is clearly requested by the parents. Many parents are already exhausted by the physical stress of having a baby. If there are other children in the family, it can also be difficult for them to get through a long ceremony. I begin by suggesting a half-hour ceremony, with an option for a longer ceremony at a later date, such as an anniversary memorial.

Some funeral celebrants focus on services for infants and children. Some decide not to provide those services. If you are going to decline infant and children's funerals, it is kind to have other names you can pass on to family who are seeking a celebrant. Reach out to other celebrants near you or nondenominational pastors who may provide funerals.

DEATHS OF PROBLEMATIC OR UNLIKED PEOPLE

Not everyone who dies is a nice person. And even nice people have problematic traits, bad judgements in their past, or poor (or nonexistent) relationships with family members. How to honor these people, what to say, and how to create a ceremony that walks the line between factual and bitter, between warm and unbelievable?

You can ask the family or coordinator if there are any times they remember, no matter how distant, when the deceased's better qualities were more obvious. Do they have any fond memories? If so, the funeral can be an acknowledgement of the loss of that version of the deceased, a recognition that while death takes a physical life, there is also a sadness for the loss of their positive qualities.

Another suggestion is to ask if there were specific roles or situations in which the deceased was better liked. Sometimes you learn that nasty relatives were wonderful co-workers or volunteers with their chosen communities, rather than in their families.

You can also ask a relative if there are things they learned from the deceased and their choices. Not snarky lessons like, "Yes, I had the decency to learn to not drink and drive," but kinder lessons like, "I learned that my mom's early life didn't really set her up to succeed. I couldn't make her life better, but I have been a better person from seeing her struggles first hand." Sometimes our own positive qualities are reactions against what we see our relatives go through. This can be a focus for funerals for difficult people.

In addition to whatever else you uncover, you can point to the humanity of struggles, challenges, weaknesses, and failures. Not many people set out to be bad. We all struggle with integrity, commitment, honesty, and ethics in various situations. As a celebrant you can clear a little space for recognizing the humanity of the deceased.

Finally, if all else fails, or if you need to "pad out" a funeral for someone difficult, you can remind people that one of the things that makes us human is our duty to mark death formally. In having a ceremony, we may not be celebrating the deeds and choices of the deceased. Instead we are reassuring ourselves of our capacity to care, our willingness to forgive in a way that restores our own wholeness, and our gracious participation in the human race.

PUBLIC FIGURES AND COMPLEX CEREMONIES

A funeral for a public figure can be a steep learning curve. Most celebrants who perform a ceremony like this had no prior experience in large or complex funerals. Your sense of your own readiness for this is the best guide. For future reference, the Appendix includes an outline of U.S. Representative John Lewis's funeral, which spanned many days and locations.[44] As a celebrant your main concerns will usually be:

- creating a meaningful whole from a wide variety of rituals and symbols;
- finding ways to involve a variety of groups; and
- logistical concerns such as weather, venue capacity, ensuring speakers can be heard, and other audio/visual needs.

LONELY FUNERALS

A ceremony where there are very few attendees, perhaps even none, can be difficult. If your celebrant ego is active, it might take a small hit. If you have not considered what parts of a ceremony feel critical in a sparsely attended funeral and which might feel overdone, you could lose your way a bit.

This is where having a basic funeral ceremony template can come in handy. You can also play around with scaled down rituals and gestures. You might never consider using candle-lighting rituals without a clear reason, but here you might include one for yourself to do, to open the ceremony and add some gravitas and respect. You might explore what it is like to conduct the ceremony standing right next to the remains of the deceased to create some personal connection, instead of conducting from a podium. You can bring formality to a ceremony just ten minutes long, instead of grasping for things to say to draw it out needlessly to thirty minutes. As Mary Oliver says, "The real prayers are not the words but the attention that comes first." Simply standing with your hand on a casket or urn for a full minute or two, attending to the deceased, can be ceremonial.

Part 4.
Doing the Work

Funeral Celebrant's Workflow

Below are many possible points of contact for funeral celebrancy work, from earliest likely contact, through the basic tasks of creating a ceremony to the final point of contact. Not all end-of-life celebrants do all elements of this work, and not all celebrants work in the same way. You will need to decide what your services, preferences, and work habits are. Consider providing a wide range of services while you build experience, and then focusing on specific offerings that work well for your overall situation.

PRE-NEED

Inquiry from an individual

Inquiries may come from someone who wants to learn about end-of-life options, create their funeral ceremony, and document/share their wishes. Sometimes the inquiry comes from a spouse who knows there will soon be a need for a funeral ceremony.

Learning, documenting, planning meeting

Prepared with the individual, a spouse/partner, or the family to share and document wishes, ideas, and plans for what to do in the immediate days after the death of the individual/client.

IMMEDIATE NEED/AT NEED/IN NEED

Inquiry from Next of Kin

Usually at this point, the deceased has already been cremated or is at a funeral home. For a home funeral, the deceased may be at home. In any case, the funeral service is happening fairly quickly.

Inquiry from funeral director/funeral home

The funeral director calls you for a specific family they think would be a good fit for you.

Family intake or inquiry

The intake or inquiry call happens after a FD has given you contact information for a family. There is a sample intake/inquiry form in the Appendix. If you decide you cannot take the job, be direct and have a few names to refer them to.

Send service agreement and arrange fee

Prepare some way to formalize the arrangement where both parties are confident about services being provided and the fees for those services. These service agreements can be much simpler than celebrant contracts for weddings. There is a sample in the Appendix. Generally, but not always, the family member who pays your fee is the person with decision-making power.

Post-inquiry

It is a good habit to update the FD on whether you will be handling the celebrant role or not. Use your judgment about when to get back in touch with them. If the ceremony is within about four days, you might want to call them, even if it is after hours, to let them know and thank them again for referring you. If the ceremony is more than four days away, you can probably drop them an email or call during your next regular business hours.

Introduce yourself to the chapel, cemetery or venue (if different from the funeral home)

During your next business hours, reach out to the venue, if different from the funeral home, to introduce yourself and let them know you will be conducting the service. Ask about their audio/visual capabilities and policies. This avoids the back and forth of meeting with a family then asking the venue what is possible. It streamlines your work effort when you can steer the family toward what is feasible.

Create a process for sharing ceremony information or shared online workspace

It can be helpful to have a place where participants upload material or work on shared elements like remembrances and eulogies. Having an online document area also streamlines your work. You spend less time asking people to submit material, and you can look over the content and tone of pieces when it is convenient for you. Keep a private folder for your writing before you share it with the family.

CREATING THE CEREMONY

Family interview

This is when you meet with the person who has rights of disposition, and sometimes extended family and close friends, in order to gather information needed to create the ceremony. There is a sample interview form in the Appendix. When I meet with large families or groups, I suggest it is helpful when one person is the point person or has decision-making power, and ask who that person is. That way I know if there are conflicts who I need to check in with. During the interview, begin creating a draft outline and seek out themes, messages, or hopes the family has for the service. In closing, let them know what they can next expect from you, and what will be required of them. Let them know how to communicate with you if they have questions, changes, or material.

Interview follow-up

After meeting with the family, put deadlines in writing, for your benefit and for the family's, and note the major ceremony elements and responsibilities you heard them request. You want to make sure you are headed in the right direction before you get down to serious writing. The time frame for many end-of-life ceremonies does not give you much room to change direction if there are misunderstandings. I also prefer having this information in writing so the family can review it at their convenience. Families are often in a daze; having choices documented can allow them to relax.

Create the outline - Do some critical thinking about the eulogy - Choose or create rituals

Unless you have learned otherwise during the family interview, assume a main funeral ceremony of about forty-five minutes from opening to closing words. Begin plugging things into your overall outline. Let your mind play with eulogy themes and concepts, seeing if any seem like a good approach for your writing. Think of a couple of rituals to suggest to the family as requested or appropriate.

Share the ceremony outline and possible rituals with NoK - Begin writing eulogy

Confirm the big elements of the ceremony and who is doing what, get feedback on any open decisions, capture any changes the family has made, and get approval on anything you have questions about. Focus especially on knowing who will be delivering the eulogy. Try to confirm the estimated lengths of all planned speeches. At some point you must forge ahead with a draft of the eulogy if you are writing it. Making a start now is helpful.

Complete a draft of the eulogy

If the NoK wants to hear the eulogy ahead of time, decide how to share it.

Follow up with funeral home and/or cemetery

Confirm details, mention any ceremony elements that impact the venue, and confirm if they are providing any typical materials the family has requested (e.g., candles, petals) or that the ceremony will need (e.g., microphones, side tables).

Complete the Ceremony

Ensure all your primary written sections are complete. Confirm the family approves any elements you suggested. Revisit your outline and make sure all the pieces will fit in the time frame allotted. Do you need more material? Or less? Now is when you must make choices, balancing the emotional needs of the mourners, the professional constraints of the venue and funeral home, and the hopes for the ceremony.

Notice for final payment

Depending on how you have arranged your billing model, you might require full payment before the funeral.

Twenty-four hours before the ceremony

Send the NoK a message about when you plan to be at the ceremony. Let them know you will check in with them to see how they are doing and coordinate any last minute changes.

AFTER THE FUNERAL

Notice for final payment

If you require payment after the funeral, you can bundle the request with the thank you rather than send multiple messages. Many funeral homes will pay you on the day of the service, but if you are billing the funeral home, send the request after the ceremony.

Thank you

A day or two after the funeral, send a thank you note or email, letting the family know your thoughts about getting to know the deceased and your hopes that the ceremony was what they wanted. If you are creating a commemorative copy of the ceremony, you can also remind them about any speeches or materials you would like copies of so you can include them.

Follow up after funeral

If you are creating a commemorative copy of the ceremony, send it within a couple of weeks after the funeral, along with a final thank you.

POST-NEED REQUESTS

Memorial service

The workflow for a memorial service will be similar to a funeral service, but you generally have longer to create the ceremony and probably will not be interacting with a funeral home. I have always received requests for true memorials directly from family and not from a funeral home. Many families opt for direct cremation/burial, and then plan a memorial service at a later date. Be aware that with direct cremations and burials, the line between funerals and memorials is increasingly blurred. Families might opt for a direct cremation, then hold a ceremony at a later date that they call a memorial, but which serves the purpose of a funeral and may even have remains present.

Milestone dates

These are key dates when the bereaved may be thinking of the deceased, such as Mother's Day, Father's Day, or a child's birthday. It is nice but not required to send a card or email. I only send one of these a year in addition to a one-year anniversary card—so two pieces of communication in the year following the death.

Anniversary of death

Sending a card or email around the one-year anniversary of the death is kind but not required. It depends on the kind of relationship you have with the family or Next of Kin.

Handling Inquiries

There are some things you can do to help inquiries go smoothly for the people you interact with and for yourself. Most revolve around the reality that many end-of-life inquiries involve a very fast turnaround for people in high levels of stress and decision making. Some suggestions for how to meet these requests efficiently and helpfully:

- If the initial inquiry was via email or phone and did not specify a date and time, update your calendar before returning the call so you are better able to confirm your availability when you return the call.
- Have a sense of your availability, and ideally have your calendar with you at all times, before returning a call so you can confirm right away.
- Call people back as soon as possible, and within an hour or two if you know you are not available. This allows them to move on quickly to find other people who are available.
- Have some other names to suggest if declining the service.
- For work/life balance: I have a phone service that allows me to forward a business number to my main phone, and also transcribes messages. This way, if it is an after-hours call, I can check if it is for a funeral and requires an immediate response.

There are a few things to sort out for yourself prior to handling inquiries with grace. Here are some.

How will you refer to the deceased? You can say "the deceased," "your loved one," "your mom," "your son," etc. Generally, I go with "your mom" or "your father's body." As you get closer to the funeral and on the day of, you might shift your language to "your dad's urn" or "the casket." The unfortunate reality of death must start somewhere and language is one of the places. None of this is a rule. There are certainly services I delivered where it felt perfectly acceptable to call the deceased by his first name for the entire ceremony, and even to joke, "Where's Sebastian?" when no one knew where the urn was. The point is to assess the family's comfort and your own so that you are not creating discomfort.

Do you have a point of view about the terms you will use for death? Are you unwilling to use terms that imply an afterlife (passed on, with the angels, lost, in Heaven, etc.)? I let my clients know that it is my practice to use the terms dead, died, death, etc., and that if they find them difficult, to let me know if they have a strong preference for other terms. But I also tell them that I find the simplicity of these terms gently admits the sad reality that someone they loved is no longer alive.

What is your comfort level with religious content of any kind? Ask the family specifically about any religious elements they would like and decide if those are ok for you to deliver, whether you are comfortable if someone else delivers them, or if you may not be a good fit for the service.

What services are you confident delivering? For instance, do you want to offer one package that includes a comprehensive ceremony, a graveside interment/committal service, and a memorial service at a later date? Or do you want to create a menu of services à la carte that families can pick and choose from? What services or elements are you willing and unwilling to do? For instance, are you willing to read prayers? Would you be able to deliver a funeral for a murderer? Will you charge for children's funerals or do them *gratis*?

Notes for Serving LGBTQ+ Families and Families of Choice

Many humanist celebrants want to be safe spaces for the ceremonies of those who may have not experienced social validation or support while alive. A key time to do this is during the inquiry conversation. You might simply say, "In case you don't know, I serve all races, faiths, orientations, and identities. And even though I don't conduct religious services, anyone may have a nonreligious service. You don't have to be a humanist."

One increasing care for celebrants is how best to serve people identifying along a spectrum of gender identities and expressions.

For ceremonies where a funeral home is involved, major choices such as names and pronouns will usually be decided before you receive an inquiry. The FD and NoK will have aligned on the name and gender identity through a combination of legal documents (such as name change and death certificates) and discussion. Where there is conflicting or absent information, funeral homes generally must follow the wishes of the person with the rights of disposition.

In cases where your main or only point of contact is the NoK, you may never know whether the identity of the deceased that has been given to you is congruent with how the deceased would have represented themselves. Some families may be confused about how to reconcile a chosen identity with a gender assigned at birth. Other families or NoK may choose to ignore the chosen identity of the deceased. And still others may not have known about the identity choices of the deceased.

When families approach you directly, you can show your friendliness and openness to serving the LGBTQ+ community by not assuming gender identity and pronouns. Ask directly how you should represent the deceased in spoken matters through their name and pronouns. Death is frequently a time when mourners reconcile a number of realities and qualities held by the deceased. By showing that you are open to the reality and language of nonbinary, trans, and other identities, you can make it easier for families to take a step toward integrating chosen identities into the ceremonial aspects of death.

If you have LGBTQ+ clients who are concerned about their ceremonial rights and wishes, you can help by directing them to up-to-date information on laws in your state and issues to consider. The best practice for people who want their wishes followed is to identify someone supportive of their choices and to assign that person the legal rights of disposition as required by the state. You can find more resources for serving the LGBTQ community in the Bibliography.

INTAKE/AVAILABILITY REQUESTS

If you have been contacted by a FD, get as many details as possible about the service from them so you can assess your ability to conduct it. You can find sample inquiry and interview forms in the Appendix for an exhaustive list of questions. If this is your first time working with this funeral home:

- determine who you will bill/invoice, either the funeral home or the family directly;
- get a sense of the complexity of the service and provide an estimate on the spot;
- capture details about the deceased: name, age, date of death, date/time/location of planned service, method of final disposition, cause of death, name and relationship of primary contact;
- ask for the best way to follow up with FD (phone, email) and get their contact details;
- ask if there are any other details they think is important for you to know;
- tell the FD you will send them basic info about you (including general pricing) and that you will be back in touch with questions or a final price after confirming ceremony details with family; and
- thank the FD for referring you to the family.

If you will be taking the role and you are unfamiliar with the funeral home, it is good to ask what their setup is for audio/visual, live-streaming, and anything else you can think might impact your ceremony design before you meet with the family for the longer interview. That way you can guide the family efficiently in creating a ceremony you can actually deliver. You can also ask the FD if there is a good time to stop by and look at the space if it will put you at ease.

When contacting a family, introduce yourself. Let the person know if a FD has referred you. Ask if it is a good time to talk. Ask for more details or confirm what you heard from the FD to get a sense of the ceremony they would like: basic details like the date, location, what kind of ceremonies they are thinking of (funeral, committal, memorial, or some combination), the tone of the ceremony, and confirm your availability and fit for the service. Many people will not know the lingo of funeral versus committal versus memorial. As a nonreligious celebrant, I find it helps to ask now about the religiousness of a ceremony: are they envisioning prayers, mention of a god, or religious rituals?

If you are hearing directly from a family for the initial inquiry, you will need to ask directly whether the body will be present for the ceremony. Many people, especially with cremations, blur the idea or the terms for funeral and memorial. You can ask, "Will your mom's remains be present?" or "Have you decided to have the casket present for the funeral service?" or "The funeral director let me know your sister was cremated so I imagine the urn with her remains will be present. Is that right?" It is important to be direct and matter-of-fact.

Decide how you are going to ask about the final disposition if it was not communicated from a FD. In my experience, most people do not know the term disposition, so you may need to proceed confidently: "And how will your dad's body be laid to rest? Will he be buried, or....?"

If you decide you cannot take the job, be clear and quick to let the family know, and have a few names to refer them to. Lack of clarity is the worst for people in this situation. They need simple, clear information and reduced choices.

If you can take the job, tell them the next steps and describe your payment policies. If you will be invoicing them directly, ask for enough details that give you a sense of what you will charge. It can be helpful to give a range over the phone during this first call if you are confident about it. Anything that lets the NoK either continue the conversation or decline and try to find someone else is helpful because the turnaround time is often so short.

Know if you will ask for a reservation fee and how/when you will require the rest of the fee. Know if you will ask families to sign a contract or not.

If you will be taking on the role of celebrant, end your conversation by agreeing on a date, time and location for a complete family interview. Note that you can often use the funeral home for conducting a family interview in situations you feel might be risky or uncomfortable in going to the home of the family. You can also ask funeral directors if there are any red flags they noticed that might incline you to meeting someplace neutral. You can also hold family interviews completely over the phone or by video conference.

If you were originally contacted by a Funeral Director, call them as soon as possible after the inquiry with the family to let them know if you will be taking the role of celebrant or not. If it is relevant, let the FD know why and thank them again for referring you.

Handling Family Interviews

After you have taken on a service for an immediate funeral, the family interview needs to happen quickly. Video interviews with families are certainly more common after the Covid-19 pandemic, but in general I find it is more informative to meet with the family in person. You will have an easier time parsing who is making the decisions, who might be pushing too hard for something, or who might not be speaking up.

In terms of taking care of the family during this significant meeting, there are a few helpful tips. One is to prepare them for what to expect. I ask them to set aside at least an hour, and sometimes up to three, to help me get to know their loved one. The length of time we meet is usually driven by the ceremony they're requesting and the lifespan of the deceased. A full funeral and a long lifespan often mean more people participating in the interview, more stories, more roles during the ceremony, and more time for you to hear and sort through stories to see what is most essential. Three hours of material will not make it into the ceremony, but hearing more than you need makes you more confident about the true characteristics of the deceased.

That doesn't mean that graveside committals for a young person always mean short, one-hour family interviews. Sometimes people are so traumatized by a death that they have a compulsion to tell and retell stories about the deceased and the impact of the death. But in terms of what you need to move forward with writing, those family interviews are usually shorter.

I also share in advance some major questions I will be asking. Some people are able to express emotions spontaneously but others are not. Participants can get anxious when they cannot develop a statement on the spot that captures their feelings. So, even though the door is open for more contributions after I leave the family meeting, it is helpful to prepare people in advance. Since time is usually tight for funerals, anything that helps make the interview productive will give you valuable time to write the ceremony.

You will have to find your own comfort zone with methods for documenting information, especially because methods change. You might ask questions spontaneously and capture everything in writing; you might record everything in a sound file for review later; you might record a video meeting; you might just listen and make notes afterwards. I tend to have my questions preprinted with large blank areas where I can write notes in the moment.

THE INTERVIEW

When you meet a family in their home or at the home of the deceased you may quite quickly become a trusted person with whom the family feels more relaxed. You may meet kids who will be less nervous on the day since they know you a bit. Because funerals often change on the fly, having a reserve of rapport built up is helpful for minimizing indecision and changes. If you suggest changes on the day of, the family is more likely to understand and accept the changes. And knowing the family, you are better able to judge which changes will be best.

For the interview itself, it is productive to start wherever the family feels most comfortable. I often ask an open-ended question such as, "What can you tell me about Jackson or the ceremony you have in mind for him?" These two major routes, about the person and about the ceremony, provide most of the ceremony information you will need. If the family is having trouble, you can ask about their favorite stories about the deceased. Photos can also help focus on cherished memories, or jog memories, and allow you to ask about different time periods in the life of the deceased. It is the same with physical objects that were either prized by the deceased, or that they were associated with (a wrench set, camera, quilts, record collection, etc.).

Based on the stories, you can follow some threads for more detail. When you hear a general statement—"He was kind/aloof/

funny"—gently probe for specifics and ask people to recall examples and stories. "Can you tell me about a time you saw Jim's kindness in action?" Like the formula for a good compliment (genuine, personal, and specific), so also are the most helpful stories about the deceased. On one hand they help the bereaved confront the scope and specificity of their loss (not just any father has died, *their* father has died), and on the other hand they help you include details that bring a ceremony alive. Alternately, when you hear specific stories, gently probe for larger life themes. "It sounds like Jim was very kind. Is that accurate?" After you have heard the family stories or have enough sense of the deceased to start writing, you can move directly to reviewing the ceremony elements and flow that make sense based on what you have heard.

If you encounter families struggling to describe the deceased or share their life story, you can instead start with what elements of the ceremony they feel most strongly about. Given that most families are overwhelmed at this time, it is helpful to have a printed sample of the elements and flow your standard funeral ceremony. As the family talks about their wishes and plans, you can mark off what makes sense and talk to them about reasons to include anything they have not mentioned. For instance, if the family has talked about the strong connection the deceased had to their birth country but there is nothing in the ceremony to acknowledge that, you can ask if it is important to include it in some way and almost immediately suggest an element or place in the ceremony that needs material. Occasionally you might suggest excluding something they want to include. Cultural or religious appropriation might be one of those reasons. Ritual overload is another reason to pare back.

Finally, you will encounter families who, for one reason or another, have no emotional bandwidth for participating in the creation of the ceremony beyond the most basic details of name, birth date, and something like the favorite rock band of the deceased. It simply may deplete a family's energy level to spend time creating a highly personalized service. That is ok. You can create and perform a simple ceremony, perhaps even one you have already created as a standard offering, with personalization in just a few spots. You can choose readings and read them yourself if no one from the family can participate. And, if you find yourself meeting resistance when asking for information, it is ok to simply suggest to the family, "This is a difficult time. I wonder if you'd prefer me to arrange the ceremony fully so you have time to just be with each other?" As I said earlier, for many people the most important aspects of a funeral are that it happened and that it's over. An "impersonal" funeral is not a bad choice. It does not indicate less love or care.

WRAPPING UP THE FAMILY INTERVIEW

When the interview is over, thank everyone for their time and for helping you get to know the deceased. People also appreciate hearing that they are doing the right thing. Whether it is "What a fun ceremony this will be—you've obviously had so much joy from knowing Kirsten!" or "This is a difficult task but what you've got in mind sounds just right." Let them know what the next steps are for you and for them so they do not have to keep more in mind than necessary.

If you are creating and reading a eulogy, give them a rough idea of when you will have a draft completed, usually twenty-four hours for immediate need services. Determine how or whether they want to hear it in advance, and make arrangements to review it together at the level you agree on.

If someone else is writing and reading eulogies, give them a deadline by which you would like to have a completed copy or (at least) a word count to help you gauge time. If you are setting up a shared online workspace, let them know you will do that and that people will have a way to contribute. Don't overload the family in person with details, however. Save that for an email or written communication so they can read it and refer back to it when they need to. Overwhelm, distraction, and forgetfulness are very common for the grieving.

One helpful aspect of using shared online workspaces is that rather than chasing people down for their contribution or feedback, everyone participating can create or upload their material. This also helps to keep an eye on the stories other people are using for their eulogy or tributes. If I see something I planned to use in my spoken parts, I will know early to hold it back and work up something else. Keep at least one folder private for yourself, as a sandbox for your writing before you share it with the family.

End with a reassuring message that the next few days may feel chaotic but that no matter what happens it will all come together and the funeral will be a loving/appropriate/personal reflection of the deceased.

AFTER THE INTERVIEW

On returning to my workspace, I quickly create an outline of the ceremony, assign responsibilities as I understand them, and put suggested deadlines in writing. Then I follow up with the family with a thank you for their time, and I share the outline with them so they can review and confirm my understanding and fill in any blanks that have become clear since we spoke. Things move quickly. You can also share any relevant links to shared workspaces and set expectations for when you each get in touch with the other.

Conducting the End-of-Life Ceremony

Practicalities for the day of the service

WHAT TO BRING AND WEAR

- A printed copy of the entire ceremony, including the eulogy (no matter who is reading it), and copies of the primary readings and speeches. I find it helpful to have two copies of each reading or eulogy; sometimes readers will forget their copy, read from yours, and then walk off with it.
- Small packet of tissues for yourself and others
- Shoes you can walk in on uneven ground and which can get muddy if doing a committal service
- Umbrella, raincoat, or whatever handy gear your climate would dictate

ON ARRIVAL AT THE CEREMONY LOCATION

The order of tasks below is one I find most helpful from the celebrant's point of view. However, you will need to be flexible based on who is available (physically and emotionally) and on the complexity of the service.

- Check in with the funeral director or main cemetery contact to let them know you have arrived. See if there are any substantial changes from their points of view that will affect you. Sometimes the family changes their mind about participating in the burial or having the casket open. Confirm with FD about the entrance/exit of the body; who, if anyone, is accompanying; the mark you will start on; and what happens after the ceremony (graveside committal, reception, etc.). Ask if there is a quiet place where you can leave your things or see if the podium will accommodate them. Confirm materials are in place.

- Check in with Next of Kin and gauge their emotions. Ask if they feel up to doing their readings or rituals as planned. Ask especially about kids. Offer to take on those readings if they do not have another person lined up. See if there are any other last-minute changes to the content of the ceremony, e.g., who will be speaking, what they are covering, who will be performing...or not. Agree on how to adjust the ceremony while in progress, for example, how will you check in about unplanned tributes, changes in the kids' willingness to participate, if a slideshow does not load as planned, etc.? Ask the Next of Kin to point out to you any main speakers you do not know.

- Introduce yourself to the main speakers/readers and let them know how you will call them up to speak when it is time. Ask if they have a printed version of their speech. If so, ask if you can photograph it. This is helpful if they decide they are unable to deliver the speech, and also for you to have a copy for a commemorative version later if you are making one.

- If it is close to the start and there are a number of empty rows, ask people to fill in the front seats.

- Go back to your quiet place and make any needed adjustments to the ceremony. If there is time, speed read others' speeches to see if any of the stories you were planning to tell are included. If so, you will want to modify them from your speaking portion. You can either transition differently to other speakers or fill in with a back-up story. Whether this is easy or not depends on your ceremony.

- Check in with musicians to make sure they are clear about when they perform, how you will cue them, and if they have checked their equipment and volume ahead of time. This is more a concern with family and friends who will be performing than for professional musicians.

- Come back to the Next of Kin and see if they are ready for you to start the ceremony. Let them know what you and they will do at the end of the ceremony. Be very clear, for example: "When the ceremony's over, the pallbearers will carry your Dad out. I'll ask you to walk directly behind your Dad. Then we'll walk to the gravesite. If you forget, don't worry, I'll say it all again at the end of the ceremony and I'll be there."

- If you are doing a graveside casketed service, discreetly check in with the grounds crew when you arrive to let them know if the casket will be lowered during the ceremony, and who will cue them to do so. Confirm for them whether the family will want a shovel to start the burial of a casket or urn. Some cemeteries have a small bowl or bucket of dirt for people to take their handful from.

- When you are finished with a graveside service, you can step aside or stand with cemetery employees to indicate that you are giving the family space to complete their goodbyes or to mingle with guests. I often stay until the guests have departed, but my body language says that the service is over.

- A note about photography and social media: I typically treat the names of the deceased and their family or friends as confidential, and do not name them in my posts. Nor do I post any images of the family, ceremony, or gravesite from the day of the ceremony. However, I usually take a photo of the gravesite after the family has left that day, or on another day when the weather or beauty are particularly dramatic. Many families seem to appreciate it when, at a later date, I tell them I have a few photos from the day or of the site, and ask if they would like me to share these with them. While I might take close-up photos to send to the family, I can often capture a few images where the name of the deceased is not visible. For me, these feel more appropriate as images for social media. You will need to find your comfort level amid the norms of your area and your communities for how you handle social media and images of funerals. There are many approaches that can work, but being clear with your clients about it is helpful for them.

Part 5.
The Business of End-of-Life Celebrancy

Business Models

To illustrate where we celebrants find ourselves in terms of professions and livelihoods, let me give a brief overview of three important historical threads of funeral work in the United States.

The first thread occurs before the mid-1800s, when most funerals were *de facto* home funerals. People died at or near home, were kept at home for viewings, were ritually prepared for burial at home, and were brought from home to a church or graveyard for rites and burial. Often family or friends made the coffin or casket and transported the body. There was very little cost for this, and burial was often covered by a family's previous tithes (or taxes) to their religious institution. The dying and funeral processes were also common family knowledge, passed down by the process of participation, at times when people experienced death more often and at younger ages.

The second thread comes in the mid-1800s, when body preservation became an urgent desire during the Civil War. Soldiers killed in action were brought home from battle fields via refrigerated train cars. A method of preserving the body was perfected. The funeral industry sprang up around these needs of transport and preservation. The responsibility for death preparation moved out of the home, away from the family, and into funeral homes and toward funeral directors. Costs were associated with these new practices. Due to social trends, money spent on funerals came to symbolize class membership, family love, and duty.

The third thread is the concentration of ceremonial power and leadership in religious institutions. Most cultures strive to understand what happens after death. Religions have proposed a variety of answers. Religious leaders therefore became the customary leaders of ceremonies designed to ensure the deceased could participate after death in whatever system their religion described. The religious leaders were, and continue to be, supported by their religious organizations. The average rabbi makes $100,775 per year.[45]

The average Catholic priest makes about $57,000 per year.[46] Religious leaders usually receive housing and travel stipends. Being fired or laid off is almost unheard of. When they conduct funeral services, therefore, they do not need to make a living wage of it, and typically receive only an honorarium (currently about $100).

The number of people who find meaning, harmony, and heart's-ease in something outside of organized or congregational religion has grown. As a result, more people are seeking out nonreligious end-of-life ceremonies. But the sense of who should lead nonreligious death rites has not kept pace with this change, and there are not similar structures where celebrants are supported and provided for by an institution or congregation. As a result, it can sometimes seem to funeral homes and families that celebrant fees are expensive or unethical. After all, to families of the deceased, religious leaders appear not to be paid at all! Where these threads join is where you find yourself as a nonreligious celebrant trying to make a living.

EMPLOYMENT MODELS

There are two main models of funeral celebrancy evolving in the United States. You are either hired on an as-needed basis or you are an employee. You may be hired on an as-needed basis by a funeral home/direction, or by the family directly. A funeral home may have you on its list of celebrants, like preferred vendors in the wedding business. Or they may have been given your name by a fellow funeral director, and they reach out to you on behalf of a family for a specific funeral. In the United States these "preferred vendors" are usually clergy members but the desire for nonreligious funeral officiants and celebrants is growing.

Depending on how you market yourself, you might also be contacted directly by a family or next of kin. In that case you would be hired directly by the family. You might also be contacted directly by the cemetery. With more dispositions being direct cremation or direct burial, sometimes the cemetery is the place where families first encounter their wish for a celebrant. Cemeteries also have lists of clergy members and celebrants they share with families.

Some funeral homes now see a clearer benefit of using a celebrant and they have either trained a member of staff as a celebrant or they hire a celebrant as an employee full- or part-time. Some celebrants I know conduct a number of ceremonies at a specific funeral home, and the funeral home is impressed enough and sees enough need for the role that the funeral home extends an offer to become an employee.

PRICING CONSIDERATIONS AND CONVENTIONS

It will be helpful for your work process, your marketing, and your scheduling to determine an à la carte approach to the various ceremonies you plan to offer, as well as some bundles of services that make sense for you and your potential clients. Some components to consider for bundling are:

- a funeral ceremony, including all the meetings with the family, creation of the ceremony, conducting the service, and travel to and from the ceremony site;
- a graveside service, and some variations of it, such as very short committal service or one that is closer to a complete funeral with elements like songs, readings, a eulogy;
- a witnessed cremation, and what that means to you and/or your local area; and
- a memorial celebration.

My personal approach has been to bundle ceremonies into meaningful packages that families in my area tend to request. But I am also able to offer *à la carte* prices as needed. Currently I bundle funerals with graveside committals (casket or urn), and funerals with witnessed cremations. Adding a memorial at a later date is something I can suggest after talking with the family, if it feels like they would appreciate one. I often do not spell out these options to the family contact. Rather I listen to what kind of ceremony they want and then propose the service or bundle that fits best, with a total price. This is based on my sense that most families do not want a list of options and add-ons, but rather want clarity and ease of decision making.

Similar to weddings, the dollar amount you can charge funeral homes and families is going to vary greatly depending on the economic reality of your area, whether there are other celebrants in your area, the religious and nonreligious population of your area, and whether you have some differentiating feature or benefit to offer. Your training is definitely a benefit. Other ideas might be having property to use for various ceremonies, having an "all-in-one" service that includes vessels, flowers, photography, etc. The ability to offer digital memorials could be helpful now as well.

One thing to recognize is that the end-of-life business space is very gendered and racially homogenous. Fifty-five percent of funeral directors are male (ten years ago it was sixty-seven percent). Eighty-two percent are white (virtually unchanged from a decade ago).[47, 48] This concentration of business control in the funeral industry is the historical effect of religious roles in the nineteenth and twentieth centuries being held almost exclusively by white men, and of racial discrimination and segregation in the the country at large, most obviously in the mid-1800s when the funeral industry got its start. In the funeral industry, that effect of religion is coupled with the heavily male-dominated funeral industry itself. Conversely, while the demographics of the death care community does not seem to be surveyed yet, in my experience there are more women than men and it seems more racially diverse. (Where the term *funeral industry* is used, it covers the licensed and professional transportation, arrangement, and disposition of bodies through funeral homes, mortuaries, cemeteries, and crematoria. *Death care community* refers to a number of death-adjacent roles such as doulas, grief companions, or even "minority"-run funeral homes that have sprung up in reaction to the needs and communities that funeral homes don't serve or don't serve well.)

As a result of this gendered reality, male celebrants I know typically charge $1000+ for funerals. Only two female celebrants I know charge more than $1000 or more for weddings, and they charge less for funerals.

Based on conversations with many women celebrants, most seem to regard funeral celebrancy and end-of-life work as a kindness for which they feel awkward or inappropriate accepting

money. Women celebrants of color can also find themselves
doing even additional unpaid labor when asked to educate their
colleagues and groups on diversity, "alternate" cultures and
traditions, and the very existence of systemic racism itself.[49] This
worsens the gender and racial wage gap they already experience.[50]
Male celebrants, on the other hand, regard end-of-life work as a
necessary and important community role for which they should be
compensated. Whether this impacts you or not will again depend
on the factors at play in your location and your personal situation.
Given that the United States economy already benefits from more
than a trillion dollars of unpaid labor by women,[51] I am in favor of
women charging a fee that reflects a living wage that contributes
meaningfully to their unique personal financial circumstances.

My pricing model is based on a target income I want to make
with celebrancy work. It might change based on whether I want
to perform more weddings in a given year, or whether my year
includes other sources of income such as teaching or writing.
After I identify my target income, I add up the number of days
per month I could potentially deliver ceremonies—for instance,
how many ceremonies on weekends in June plus weekday funeral
services. Dividing the target income by the number of ceremonies
gives me a rough idea of what I should try to charge per ceremony.
Then the issue becomes how many hours it takes to attract clients,
and the work-hours needed to create and deliver each service.

One celebrant I know uses a pay-what-you want sliding scale.
For her it works very well; she is the lone celebrant in a populated
but remote area, with a very diverse population. When people ask
about the cost of her services, she gives them a range from the most
she has ever been paid (around $1500) to free. She then lets people
judge for themselves where they are on that scale. Because she is
one of the only celebrants in her area and because she is part of a
tight-knit community, this works well for her. Here in the metro
Boston area, a group of celebrants I network with think this model
would begin to set us up to compete against each other invisibly.

One last thing to consider is that it is a convention among
funeral celebrants to provide infant and child funerals at no charge.
However, some celebrants focus their practice completely on infant

and child funerals and do charge. It's helpful to think about your approach to this practice before you get a request, and what age ranges this encompasses.

There are many different models that may work for you, and probably others I have not even considered. You are encouraged to navigate toward what works for you!

PROPOSAL AND CONTRACTING

With funeral homes, you will generally invoice them before or after the ceremony. After a certain dollar amount of payment to you, they may issue you a tax form or you may need to claim the amount for taxes. Again, your own financial situation will determine what is best for you, so you should talk with someone knowledgeable about it. You should feel comfortable proposing plainly the invoicing/payment model you prefer, and talk with an FD about an arrangement that will work for both of you.

If you are working directly with a family, it is helpful to give them an estimate during your initial intake call, or you can let them know you will get back to them with a more precise fee in an hour or two. Then you can send them a proposal/service agreement, which lets you agree on the scope of the services and begin the contractual arrangement.

The proposal can, and I believe should, be relatively direct and short. You need simply to reiterate important elements you heard on the inquiry call, and be clear about anything your ceremony will not include (materials, travel, etc.). You can see a sample service agreement in the Appendix.

Over time, I have chosen to use a very short proposal/service agreement compared to my wedding officiant contract. One reason for this is that the role of funeral celebrant has no legal impact on you, the family, or the process, so the stakes are lower for everyone. (Unless you are planning to provide home funerals. If that is the case you must explore your state laws about any regulations on handling or transporting human remains.)

But another reason for simple contracts is that decision fatigue and overwhelm are common for families planning funerals.

Personally, I do not think end-of-life events are the time for celebrants to offer many add-ons, complicated conditional choices, or flourishes that show off your capabilities. If those are part of your work, it may be best if they are built into a flat fee. A streamlined service agreement in plain language allows the Next of Kin to make an informed choice easily, without a lot of deliberation and detailed reading, while also protecting you from nonpayment as much as a detailed contract would. Your geographic area or cultural groups may do things differently, however, so explore how you can position yourself to be of most service to your likely families.

Many celebrants, in addition to or instead of a proposal, provide the family with a document that describes "My Commitment to You" or "What You Can Expect from Working with Me." It lists some of their professional standards in delivering a funeral service in line with what the family is requesting. That is another way you could approach formalizing the arrangement.

As a reminder, the overall funeral industry is changing quite a bit, so if there is a way you want to do things differently that benefits you and your potential customers, by all means go for it!

Connecting with Community

Being part of a constellation of care for families

NETWORKING, MARKETING, AND WHERE YOU FIT IN YOUR COMMUNITY

It can feel uncomfortable to talk about marketing and networking when death is what causes your phone to ring or email to chime. However, your role as a celebrant is a comfort and beacon for one of the most important human rituals, so letting people know you exist is helpful. You can also be of more help and guidance to families if you are aware of or integrated with others in the field.

The two main domains to be a part of or network with are the funeral industry and the death care community. Whether you orient yourself as someone in the funeral industry or the death care community may be a function of your gender, training, lived experience, pricing strategies, training, professional goals, and position in your community, rather than any explicit labeling. The role of celebrant seems equally at home in both groups at this time, able to connect with families directly to support them and plan ceremonies, and to contract with funeral homes seeking officiants for the families they serve.

There is useful information and camaraderie in both realms, and in some ways it is an artificial difference. An end-of-life doula may help families prepare a loved one in their last days and then coordinate with a funeral director for transporting the body. That funeral director might coordinate with a green burial service and with you as a funeral celebrant. Most importantly, families may interact with people in all kinds of roles. They don't care how the paradigms are defined as long as their experience is supportive, warm, professional, and seamless.

In the **funeral industry**, learning from and connecting with the following groups may be helpful.

- Funeral homes - Share your name, contact information, and services with them, getting to know which FDs are aware of options like home funerals, green burials, "transport only," etc.
- The National Funeral Directors Association - They provide several articles, data, and trends about funerals, and a good way to understand business challenges your local FD may face.
- Cemeteries - Share your name, contact information, and service options with them.
- Green burial locations - Ask for a tour and explanation of their policies.
- Your local cemetery commission or Department of Public Works - Stay informed about current laws, policies, and changes at a very local level.
- Parklands and outdoor venues that accept ash scattering – Know their policies and procedures.
- Universities and research institutions that accept cadavers for education - You can either be a resource for families who are considering this option or a celebrant for memorial events at the organization.
- Burial at sea - Introduce yourself to a local provider and be a connection for families.

In the **death care community**, learning from and connecting with the following groups may be helpful:

- Organizations supporting marginalized groups' experience of death and grief - These can include groups that center the Native/Indigenous experience, the Black experience, LGBTQIA experience, and the indigent experience. You might also seek out groups who see funeral services as paths to environmental justice and financial justice.
- Nursing homes and hospice groups - You can connect with nursing homes to do educational events, give residents end-of-life forms, or give slide shows about green burial, alternative containers that can be decorated, shrouds, etc.

- Grief therapists, trauma support, counselors
- End-of-life doulas, death doulas – They support the dying and their families at the threshold of death and may be involved with physical or emotional support.
- Home funeral providers/educators
- Home funeral advocacy groups
- Green burial locations, conservation burial locations, and support/advocacy groups for those options
- DIY funeral suppliers like alternative caskets, shrouds, etc.
- Death cafes, The Five Wishes, or Death over Dinner - Organizations that provide starter conversations and materials for talking about death with your family, friends, or other communities.
- Other funeral celebrants in your area, to observe or as backup for each other.

Funerals are becoming more like weddings or other celebratory events in that meaningful venues, photographers, and event design companies might be involved. If there is a strong hobby demographic in your community you might seek out connections with venues that would be interested in expanding their event services for end-of-life celebrations and memorials.

Similarly, because so many families are geographically dispersed, funerals may be some of the only events where the majority of the family will be together for some time. You could consider connecting with a few family photographers to see if they are interested in shooting funerals or receptions.

Based on your own values and time, you might get involved at a local or state level on legislation supporting the right-to-die with dignity/assisted death, allowing disposition by newer methods like alkaline hydrolysis and composting, or the right for families to handle all matters relating to the deceased without a Funeral Director. Your local area will have its own laws, trends, and needs.

Finally, keep your eyes open for unconventional ways to connect with your community. One year I took part in my city's "Parking Day" where local businesses take over parking spaces and make them inviting places for pedestrians to hang out. I set out a few chairs and plants, and handed out information about home funerals and copies of Massachusetts Health Care Proxy forms and Order of Life Saving Treatment ("do not resuscitate") forms. It was a real conversation starter.

The Future of Funerals

Funerals are at a tipping point of new options and creativity.
Here are some recent trends.

Changes in the Demographics of the Funeral Industry

More than sixty percent of current mortuary students are women and come from outside a family business funeral home.[52] Among current funeral directors, 45% are women, versus 32% just a decade ago. By race, 7% of funeral directors are Latino or Hispanic, 6% are Black or African American, and 2% are Asian.[53] Because of segregated religious histories, the funeral industry also remains very segregated but there are more and more examples of people committed to it changing.[54] Funeral directors of all races tend to be younger if they are women, and older if they are men.[55] LGBTQ funeral directors are just 15% of all FDs. [56]

The Intersection of Death, Environmentalism, and Real Estate

Physically accommodating the dead is becoming a space problem in many places,[57] and solutions for what we do with our dead have shifted. Locations with dwindling space and/or a high cost of real estate tend to drive changes and innovations in disposition methods,[58, 59] whereas in places with an abundance of space and/or low costs of real estate, death practices tend to overlap with land conservation.[60] Local climate also has an impact on how we accommodate the dead, and local climates are changing.

Personalization and Decolonizing the Death Experience

The United States is increasingly diverse. By 2044 Black Americans, Latinos, and Asian Americans are predicted to make up a majority of the population.[61] Recognition in American death care of people who have been historically sidelined is becoming more common, and more expected, as people bring their values and lived experiences to end-of-life concerns. Communities bring a variety of histories, social customs, institutional oppressions, and therefore, a variety of needs, to end-of-life choices. You may encounter people who want to die fabulously[62] and others who are working toward end-of-life experiences unimpeded by historical oppressor norms.[63]

Personalization can now be found in all steps of the end-of-life process, from having choices about where to have your dying days, to dispositions, to ceremonial settings, and even multi-sensory experiences during the funeral ceremony.[64] However, most of the funeral industry is still dated and there is a lot of room for creativity, innovation, and change.[65]

Technology

One way that end-of-life practices are leaping ahead is in technological and digital innovation. The Covid-19 pandemic, which began in 2020 and is currently in its third year, has had an outsized impact on the funeral industry.[66] Images of mass burials and refrigerated trucks for containing bodies were surreal interruptions of our "normal" way of death. In many places, end-of-life services continued and even rose to the occasion as technology came to the foreground for ceremonies. Technology has also impacted funerals in terms of mourning, ritualizing, and remembering the dead, from grief bots[67] and ritual robots,[68] to live streaming funerals[69] and digital afterlives.[70]

Aside from the more futuristic possibilities, there is also the mundane but important step of deciding what to do with "digital remains" such as photos, email, passwords, and social media accounts. People are increasingly aware of the importance of addressing these artifacts of life, whether out of concern for privacy or simply to figure out what to delete and what to keep. Organizations now offer checklists and consulting for how to handle this element of death, for both the dying and those left behind.

Economic Factors

Industry regulation, rising personal debt, and declining disposable income levels have all combined so that people are more attentive to the true costs of funerals. White Baby Boomers may be the last cohort for some time who can afford a conventional funeral without going into debt.[71, 72] Younger generations (those now younger than sixty years old) are making more affordable end-of-life choices out of choice or necessity. Whether the popularity of new dispositions such as aquamation and natural organic reduction (NOR) spur funeral homes to offer them at competitive prices remains to be seen.

Design and Aesthetics

Many people want their end-of-life events and ceremonies to be an opportunity for beauty, harmony, and symbolism. They consider the architecture and design of funerals outdated, unpleasant, and off-putting and look for settings and elements that reflect a different taste from the funeral homes and rituals of the mid-1900s. People from a wide variety of disciplines, from architecture to biology, now have members engaging with end-of-life design challenges out of personal or professional need.[73]

The Rise of the Nonreligious and "Nones"

As the demographics in the United States shift away from organized religion, rituals associated with religion are also being reassessed. In some cases ritual, and the mourning practice of the funeral, are being abandoned altogether. In other cases, people are choosing to create new practices and rituals to take their places.

The Customer Experience and Everything Under One Roof

Our society currently places a high value on convenience. As a result, many people expect or want their end-of-life needs to be met in one place. Also, technology has the ability to confuse and to clarify end-of-life issues that many people experience for the first time, often when they are in high states of need. Companies, consortiums, and websites hope to offer end-of-life consumers "one stop shopping" for many needs.[74]

Generational Impact

Much has been written about the size of the Baby Boomer generation (born between 1946-1964) and its interest in challenging and changing traditions. Baby Boomers often have the savings, the interest, the cultural mindset, and the motivation of advancing age to shake up the funeral industry. Most have already buried their parents, and therefore bring informed opinions to how they want to do things differently. Gen X (born between 1965-1980) has been described as reluctant to be labeled, financially squeezed, comfortable with new technology, and cynical about large-scale institutions. Given the number of Baby Boomers, Gen Xers may have a lot of experience with funerals by the time they begin thinking of their own. Millennials (born between 1981-1996, ages 26-41) are a larger generational cohort than any other,[75] and will influence major life events in as yet unknown ways. However, there are signs that their attitudes about the end of life are "death positive."[76] and their choices are influenced by care for the environment and concerns for financial security.

Part 6.
Appendix

Glossary of Terms

Alkaline hydrolysis ("aquamation," "chemical disposition" "resomation") – A water and chemical mix returns the body to its primary liquid and chemical components with a uniform ash result.

Arrangement conference – When families meet with a funeral director to talk about wishes for the funeral and disposition.

Ash scattering (sometimes: strewing) – A final disposition of cremated remains outdoors.

Bier – The platform that the casket rests on during visitation and the funeral ceremony (also: catafalque).

Burial – Also called interment. Burial in the earth is the most traditional method for final disposition.

Burial at sea – Final disposition of a body at sea; many federal and maritime laws affect this.

Catafalque – The platform that the casket rests on during visitation and the funeral ceremony (also: bier).

Celebrant – A trained professional who creates and leads personalized ceremonies for life's major milestones and "events that happen only once." In the United States, celebrants generally serve nonreligious, interfaith, or "spiritual-not-religious" people who seek ceremonial support, experience, and professionalism for major life events.

Cenotaph – A monument that commemorates someone who is buried elsewhere.

Columbarium — An above-ground building or receiving wall for disposition of cremated remains.

Commendation — A spoken part of the funeral when the deceased is addressed directly. Historically it was bundled with the committal, and at this point people use the term interchangeably.

Committal service — A ceremony held at the gravesite with the casket or urn present and ending when it is lowered into the ground or immured. It commits the deceased to either their final form (for instance body to ashes) or to the final place of rest (for instance, scattered).

Conservation cemetery — Conservation cemeteries are lands set aside specifically or completely for natural burials. They are called conservation cemeteries because the needs of land conservationists and green burials often overlap. Seeing a way to satisfy both needs, groups began identifying land to conserve, and folded green burials into the purpose and mission. In addition to making natural materials a centerpiece of how remains are transported and buried, conservation cemeteries may prohibit non-natural materials for grave markers or motorized vehicles for transportation to the burial site (though many cemeteries are beginning to factor in accessibility needs).

Cortege — A funeral procession, usually in cars, from the ceremony location to site of final disposition.

Cremation — Reducing the body through heat to remains of ashes. Direct cremation is directly from the place of death to cremation without ceremony. Witnessed cremation occurs after or as part of a ceremony.

Cremation casket — A casket that will be burned as part of the cremation. Usually less formal than one used for a visitation or funeral. (Also called cremation container or alternative container.)

Cremains — The ashes and substrate left after cremation; a variation on "remains" of a dead body.

Crematory — The place where the retort is used to dispose of human remains by burning. Some crematoriums are very industrial. Others have chapels attached for witnessed cremations.

Cryomation ("Promession") — Freeze-drying the body and reducing it to particles afterwards. Not currently in use anywhere, and not fully tested.

Crypt — A burial site in a mausoleum.

Death care community — The growing number of death-adjacent roles, such as doulas, grief companions, or funeral homes run by non-traditional directors, that have sprung up in reaction to the needs and communities that funeral homes don't serve or don't serve well.

Direct burial — When the deceased is transported directly from place of death to burial without ceremony.

Direct cremation — When the deceased is transported directly from place of death to cremation without ceremony.

Disposition — The range of ways the human body is brought to its final place of rest: burial, cremation, scattering, etc. (I tend to use "place of rest" in the sense of Newton's First Law of Motion, rather than "a peaceful repose.")

Donation to science — When people give their bodies, in whole or part, to research institutions with the goal of forwarding scientific work.

Embalming — A method of preserving bodies chemically after death.

Entombment — Placing a casket in a mausoleum.

Eulogy — The main spoken part of a funeral ceremony, where speakers describe and honor the deceased.

Family room — A room at a funeral home where mourners can have privacy before, during, or after ceremonies or funeral rituals.

Final rites — The funeral service. "Rites" can refer to religious rituals, but the term is used more generally to mean the specific actions we take as humans to prepare and transition our dead to their final places.

First call (also, Transport, Removal) — When the funeral home arrives at the place of death to take the deceased from there to wherever the deceased will next be going (crematory, funeral home, burial ground, etc.). Note that in most states it is legal for NoK to do this themselves, but it is often bureaucratically burdensome for them to get the permit.

Funeral — A commemorative ceremony held at the end of a person's life to mark their passing and honor them, at which their remains are present in some form.

Funeral director (FD) — A trained and licensed person who provides for the removal of the deceased from the place of death, prepares the body, and files death certificates. Also known as a mortician or undertaker.

Funeral home (previously known as the mortuary) — The main business profession that handles human remains. The funeral home is usually multi-purpose with areas for physical preparation, holding, and ceremonies.

Funeral industry — Refers to the licensed business and professionals who handle the transport and disposition of bodies through funeral homes, mortuaries, and cemeteries.

Funeral procession — The procession from the ceremony to the committal site. See also cortege.

Green/natural burial — No embalming or effort to "preserve" the body in green or natural burials. Interment (burial) is in a conservation cemetery, hybrid cemetery, or on private land.

Grave liner — A concrete or metal container which is placed over a casket before burial, usually to help with landscaping needs.

Grave marker — A burial marker, monument, headstone, tombstone to mark the location of the grave.

Graveside service — A brief service, done after a formal funeral or instead of a formal funeral, where the body is laid in the ground. Also called a committal service.

Headstone — A burial marker, monument, tombstone, grave marker.

Honorarium — A fee typically paid to clergy for providing a ceremony.

Hybrid cemetery — Hybrid cemeteries accept green/natural burials and conventional burials. Plots for green burial may be intermingled with conventional plots in some way, or set aside in an area used only for green burials.

In state — Describes the presentation of the body for viewing before or after a funeral service ("lying in state"), usually for a person of note such as a political or cultural figure.

Inter/interred — To place a body into the ground for burial.

Interment — The activity and sometimes ceremony related to placing a body into the ground for burial. (Note: *internment* is when people are imprisoned for political or military reasons. Bodies are *not* interned and graveside services are *not* internments.)

Inurnment – Cremated remains are placed in an urn.

Lawn crypt – A dedicated underground area in a cemetery used to hold multiple human remains (a pathway, for instance).

Lowering device – Heavy machinery or mechanism used to lower the casket into the grave.

Mausoleum – A small above-ground building in a cemetery for holding entombed remains.

Memento urns – Aesthetically appropriate urns where survivors may keep all or some portion of the cremains of their loved one. Sometimes called a keepsake urn.

Memorial marker – A monument or other physical object dedicated to the memory of the deceased and placed or used in a meaningful way, like a brick in a museum's walkway, or a plaque in a garden.

Memorial service – A ceremony to mark someone's death and to honor them, generally without the body present in any form, and often held some time after the formal funeral.

In need / at need / pre-need – Describing where in the death and dying process someone might inquire. In need and at need mean that someone has an immediate need for services. Pre-need means that someone is proactively planning.

Next of Kin (NoK) – Often the term used for the person who has the legal right to make decisions about the disposition and funeral.

Niche – Recesses in a columbarium or burial sites in a garden (niche garden) where urns containing cremated remains are placed.

Obituary – A notice in the newspaper announcing a death to the community.

Order of Service (OOS) - The elements of ceremony listed in order, often printed as a booklet or pamphlet.

Pallbearers — People who carry the casket from the ceremony to the hearse and from the hearse to the gravesite. Honorary pallbearers might walk with the casket but do not actually carry it.

Plot — An area in a cemetery used for the burial of human remains.

Recomposition — Natural, organic reduction of the human body to usable soil after about thirty days.

Removal (also transport, first call) — When the funeral home arrives at the place of death to take the deceased from there to wherever the deceased will next be going (crematory, funeral home, burial ground, etc.). Note that in most states it is legal for NoK to do this themselves, but it is often bureaucratically burdensome for them to get the permit.

Retort — Cremation chamber, an industrial furnace designed to turn human remains to ash.

Right of disposition — The right to make decisions about how to handle the remains of the deceased.

Sky burial/scaffolding/tree graves — Disposition by various methods of raising the body above-ground where it will be food for birds or otherwise decompose at the effect of the weather.

State room/receiving room — The room in a funeral home where the family receives visitors and where the body is displayed for viewing or visitation.

Tomb — A place for holding remains, usually built into the landscape.

Tombstone — Another older term for a burial marker, monument, headstone, grave marker.

Transport (also removal, first call) – When the funeral home arrives at the place of death to take the deceased from there to wherever the deceased will next be going (crematory, funeral home, burial ground, etc.) Note that in most states it is legal for NoK to do this themselves, but it is often bureaucratically burdensome for them to get the permit.

Undertaker – see Funeral Director.

Urn – A small container or vessel for holding cremated remains.

Urn vault – An above-ground container for holding urns, usually for an individual or family, versus a communal columbarium which is for the cemetery as a whole.

Vault – An above-ground container for one or more deceased.

Vigil – Maintaining a presence with the body of the deceased, or immediately preceding death. Vigil has religious connotations for some, who may think it will be a prayer service.

Visitation – A scheduled time to see and pay respects to a person who died.

Wake – See Visitation.

Witnessed cremation – A cremation that occurs after or as part of a ceremony, usually partially in view of attendees.

Sample Inquiry/Intake Form

Date of Call
Contact Name   FD or relationship to the deceased?
Phone   Email
Alternate contact
Who has rights of disposition?

Funeral Home	About the Ceremony
FD/FH Contact:	Ceremony date & time
Phone number:	Ceremony place
Email:	Viewing? Y/N Public/private?
Who will invoice the family?	Venue Phone
Estimate: $	Venue contact

Moments for ceremony, and final disposition (choose all that apply):

- ☐ Home vigil
- ☐ Shrouding
- ☐ Home funeral
- ☐ Viewing at funeral home (casket open/closed)
- ☐ Funeral at funeral home
- ☐ Funeral at cemetery, chapel, or other
- ☐ Direct cremation
- ☐ Direct burial
- ☐ Interment/graveside service
- ☐ Witnessed cremation
- ☐ Ash scattering
- ☐ Burial at sea
- ☐ Military funeral
- ☐ Funeral for miscarriage
- ☐ Green burial
- ☐ Online funeral
- ☐ Celebration of Life
- ☐ Memorial

About the Deceased
Full name of deceased
Nickname
Date of death
Date of birth
Age at death
Pronouns/gender identity

Is there an obituary they can share?
Other significant information or sensitivities? Traumatic death, constraints, discordant family, etc.?
Proposed date, time and location for complete family interview:

Sample Service Agreement

Dear [NAME],

    Thank you for contacting me as a celebrant for your [relative]'s funeral. The service you're thinking of sounds very [description]. [Try to describe the tone you've understood.] I wanted to confirm in this letter and service agreement what you shared during our conversation so that I can quickly begin creating the service. If there's anything that seems amiss or if I've misunderstood any aspect of the ceremony, please get back to me as soon as possible so we can clarify.

Description of services:
- Creating and conducting a funeral ceremony in honor of NAME on Month, XX, 202X with the ceremony to start at 00:00 am/pm, and to be held at Venue Name and Address.
- The ceremony will be approximately 45 minutes long, and will be followed immediately by a graveside committal service, of approximately 10 minutes, at Cemetery Name and Address
- Preparation for the ceremony will include an interview with you, as well as the family and friends of the deceased as necessary. Please plan on at least one hour and up to three hours for this conversation, depending on the size of your family and the ceremony you envision.
- Coordinating with FD at Name of Funeral Home; and with Name at Name of Cemetery
- Additional materials for the rituals you mentioned aren't included in the fee below. I can provide guidance on where to purchase the [ITEMS] or can purchase them for you and provide a receipt.
- Travel is included in the fee quoted below. Generally I provide my own transportation to the service and between locations.
- Creating a commemorative printed version of the funeral service for you to keep

Your description of the ceremony leads me to think it will be attended by a large number of people. We talked briefly about sharing some of NAME's interests and hobbies through a community ritual. And I know that you would very much like PERSON to perform some live music. We also talked briefly about some possible readings and recorded music. I can share my current library with you online, and we can talk more about what pieces will reflect NAME's life well.

If the information above reflects our conversation and you'd like to move forward, please sign below and provide the reservation fee so I can hold the date.

You are carrying out a difficult but honored role, and I commend you for taking this step of care for your [RELATIVE]. I look forward to getting to know [NAME] through your eyes and to creating a funeral service that you and your family can look back on with peace. Thank you again for reaching out to me.

Sincerely,
   Your name here

Fee: $XXX.oo, not including costs for materials. Receipts for any additional costs will be provided to you, and I will alert you if expenses will exceed an amount of your choosing.

Payment Policy: A reservation fee of [$XXX.oo or XX%] is required to guarantee my availability for the funeral service and for me to begin the work. The remainder is due 48 hours after the completion of the service. Please see below for payment methods.

Payment method
Links to Stripe/Paypal/Square/Venmo etc.

This Letter of Agreement is agreed and accepted by

Name (Next of Kin)   Date

Name of Celebrant   Date

Enc: [any links or copies to a code of ethics or commitment of service, for example]

Sample Interview Form

Date and time of interview:
In attendance and relationship to deceased:
Is the person with rights of disposition present?

Key Details About The Deceased
Pronouns/gender identity
Maiden Name
Name known by
Age at death
Date and place of death
Cause of death/circumstances? To mention in the ceremony?
Donations? Y/N

Full Details About The Deceased

DoB:	Place Of Birth:
Spouse 1	Spouse 2
Other meaningful relationships:	
Mother	Father
Brothers: (age)	Brothers' Partners' Names
Sisters: (age)	Sisters' Partners' Names
Children: (age)	Children's Partners' Names
Grandchildren (age)	

Questions For Nok/Family
- What will this funeral service mean for your family? Do you want primarily to celebrate the life and legacies of NAME, or is this service most important to you as a time to express your grief and loss?

- Do you have photos of the deceased and can you tell some stories about them?
- What are the most important parts of the ceremony for you? Common answers might be: celebrating my loved one's life, getting the day behind us and moving on, seeing everyone, honoring the impact my loved one had on the community, gathering family, an expression of our family values, giving everyone a chance to express their love, etc.
- Did the deceased have any funeral or ceremony wishes?
- Are there faith traditions, cultural traditions, or family traditions to incorporate?
- If there is interest in any religious content to the ceremony, who is a good person for that role?
- Are there any things that honor or exemplify the deceased's personality or interests? For instance, displaying quilts for a quilter, having beloved pets attend, everyone wearing the favorite color of the loved one, hobbyist representation...
- Would you like anyone to speak at the ceremony...memories, tributes, etc.?
- Are there people you would like to thank for their support, such as healthcare workers, etc.?
- Are there people whose involvement you would like to minimize?
- Did your loved one have any favorite music, songs, readings, or quotes that immediately come to mind?
- Are there difficult or sensitive situations to be aware of?
- Will the deceased's body/remains be present in any way, and how?
- How involved do you want to be in creating the ceremony? How much interest or energy do you have for decision making?

CEREMONY ELEMENTS AND FLOW

Element	Y/N/M	Details: who, notes, materials or technical needs?
Background music for arrival		Venue is usually responsible for music, sound, audio, but not always.
Housekeeping announcements		
Opening music, perhaps standing		
Formal entry of the body or family		
Opening words from the celebrant		
Symbolic ritual		
Military honors		
Ritual for family		
Ritual for community		
Cultural, traditional, personal ritual?		
Reflection music or soundscape		Confirm the sound system in advance.
Slideshow		Confirm the AV system in advance.
Words of comfort		
Readings, poems, or spiritually moving pieces		
Reading of obituary		
Eulogy 1, 2, 3		
Planned remembrances?		
Spontaneous remembrances?		
Photo and video memories		Confirm the AV system in advance and ask about formats that can be used.

Documenting the funeral		Some families are beginning to do this with photographers or videographers.
Commendation		
Music		
Moment of silence		
Celebrant summary and close		
Donations announcement		
Reception announcement		
Other announcements?		How does the family want to be interacted with after the ceremony? Time alone, reception, gathering the next day?
Recessional music		
Physical gift for guests		
For committal service, does the family want to be present?		
Does the family want to participate in the burial (shoveling/casting dirt)?		
Other		

GETTING TO KNOW THE DECEASED

- Early life and family (parents' occupations, childhood interests, where lived)
- Education, schools, institutions, and years of attendance
- Trade, profession, work life
- Military experience
- Cultural, family, or religious traditions that you'd like to honor somehow?
- Relationships and marriage (names and dates)
- Children and family life

- Interests and activities
- Daily rituals and self comfort
- Passions, values, causes, ideals, service organizations
- Most noticeable character traits of the deceased?
- What was important to your loved one?
- What do you think NAME's definition of love was?
- What was their outlook on life and how it should be lived?
- What brought them peace, what made them happiest?
- Main turning points of their life? Roads taken and not taken?
- What important lessons do you think NAME learned in life?
- What did s/he do with their partner?
- Who are friends? You can ask friends how they met the deceased and what drew them into friendship?
- What did s/he do with friends?
- Did your loved one maintain any traditions, rituals, idiosyncrasies, or habits that defined them?
- Flaws and challenges?
- Were there any events in their life that really changed them, or created real struggle?
- Quotes that your loved one liked or lived by
- Music, books, film, the arts
- Recreation, hobbies, sports, clubs
- Charitable support
- Likes and dislikes
- Accomplishments
- Specific places that you associate with your loved one
- Greatest heartaches and regrets of the deceased
- Greatest joys
- Impact on your life on a daily level
- What will you miss the most about NAME?
- What is their legacy in your hearts?
- Dress style requests (for celebrant or others)

Sample Ceremony Outline

Below is an actual (deidentified) funeral ceremony outline. This is what I use on the day of the ceremony to see what is going to plan and what needs to change. Your outline will be different because it will be for a different person and it will be created by you.

PRE-CEREMONY SETUP AND NOTES

- Urn with Maddox's remains will already be present and placed at the front of the room among flowers
- There should be an area with two candles there, and matches at the lectern
- On arrival, check in with Nate (FD), test the mic, and place water and tissues at the lectern
- Check that Steph and Bea are prepared to perform and the mics and instruments are ready
- The family would like me to announce when it is time to be seated, and will file in to take their seats
- At the end, Karl will take responsibility for taking the urn to the reception

PROPS LIST

- Small table
- Four candles (two, and two backups), matches

What	When	Who	Notes
Music	10:30am	FD Me	Background music. Chosen by Karl, handled by FD Ask for music to be turned OFF to signal the start of the ceremony

What	When	Who	Notes
Housekee-ping	10:55am	Me	Remind people of the assistive hearing option.
Ceremony start/Music	11:00am	FD Me	Wayfaring Stranger, instrumental only - 4:52 - PLAY TO END for entrance of family. I will nod to Karl, Anna, spouses and their kids to enter and be seated.
Main Ceremony	11:02	Me	Welcome, and Opening Words
Family Ritual	11:07	Grandkids Arlo and Van, with Karl and Anna	Lighting the Candle / approx. 3 minutes Signal with Karl about whether Arlo and Van are feeling up to this. If not, Karl and Anna will light the candles.
Music	11:10	Performed by Steph and Bea	*Adventure of a Lifetime* by Coldplay, live acapella. Funeral home is providing mics. Check with Burt & Karl to ensure they're ready to read their eulogies
Reading and transition to Brian	11:13am	Me	*Mountain Thoughts*, by John Muir / 91 words
Reading	11:15am	Read by nephew Brian	*All Nature Has a Feeling*, John Clare/ 70 words
Transition to eulogies		Me	
Eulogy 1 & Transition	11:16	Me	Life outlook / 1200 words
Eulogy 2	11:23	Brother Burt	Maddox's life as a kid, by brother, Burt / 1300 words Transition if needed
Eulogy 3	11:31	Son Karl	Maddox's life as a father / 700 words

What	When	Who	Notes
Reading	11:36	DIL Kalia	*A Door to the Unknown* by anonymous / 180 words
Reading	11:37	Eddie Hart	*Sleeping in the Forest*, Mary Oliver / 180 words
Reading	11:38	Jorge	*The Body Electric* by Walt Whitman / 180 words
Music	11:39	Live by Steph Oudissia	*Wishes*, by Steph Oudissia, If it's before 11:40am, signal with Karl about whether the family is up to including spontaneous tributes.
Spontaneous remembrances	11:41	Various	Until 11:45am if there's time, but at 11:45am we need to begin wrapping up
Silent reflection & Commendation	11:46	Me	
Family Ritual	11:48am	Kids, Karl,	Extinguishing the candles
Closing message	11:49	Me	Reminder announcement Words of peace, community, joy, remembrance
Music	11:51am	FD	*Didn't He Ramble*, Glen Hansard, played by funeral home on their music system.
Community gift	NA	FD	Candles available at exit for friends and family
			Karl will be responsible for the urn after service

Sample Committal Outline

Include, exclude, and move these elements around as needed to fit your situation

The body is arranged somehow at the site. If it is an urn, often the NoK will place it on a provided table or plinth when they arrive. This is a good moment for a small gesture. It may sound strange, but I often simply bow my head toward it and say, "Pleased to meet you, NAME." If it is a casket, the placement is done by the FD as or before the mourners arrive. If everything's happening at once, the FD may get the body into place over the burial site while the family supports each other or finds seating. Sometimes mourners simply watch while the body is arranged. While things are getting situated, chat discreetly with the grounds crew to ensure your understanding of what will happen to the body and when. If the family will participate in the burial, let the grounds crew know and confirm it is ok.

1. If you are coming from a funeral service, transitional words are helpful to re-settle people. If the committal is the only ceremony, I offer brief opening words.
2. Consider perhaps a poem or reading about death, loss, transition, transformation. Music is rarer but this is also a fine moment for it instead of a poem, unless it is Taps, which is the last element.
3. Be the voice of reality and state what the purpose is here. Literally say some version of: "We are here to commit Hollis to their final resting place." You might comment on the physical space, the season, the location somehow. It's acceptable to be a little flowery, or connect it to the person's personality, or say why it is appropriate. This is a moment when validating the family's choices is kind.

4. Give a one to two minute recap of the deceased in the past tense. Speak on behalf of the mourners and do not be afraid to state the obvious at this difficult moment: "She was loved so, so much and there's no way around it: there will be a great deal of sadness in missing her." Gentle humor is ok.

5. Say a little about the physical transformation. An example: "Through the process of fire Willow's body has been purified and transformed into the simpler, ultimate elements of the universe. In committing his ashes to this ground, think again of all he meant to you and means to you."

6. A song could go here, if it is personally meaningful to the family.

7. Give the commendation, this time saying more plainly that you are releasing this person's bodily remains to the earth/fire/ air/universe/beyond. You can personalize this too, describing the deceased as being "on to their next chapter" or "taking the grandest adventure of all," etc.

8. As a final or only ritual, laying of flowers is traditional but not required. A spoken call-and-response between you and the guests can work, too.

9. Acknowledge the family's completion of this difficult step. Honor their presence for this human duty. Encourage them to support each other or tell stories about the deceased, or whatever feels right for this particular family and group as you send them on their way.

10. End the service with reminders about any event afterwards. Tell those gathered that the service is over.

Online End-of-Life Services

Online end-of-life ceremonies are new services arising out of both necessity (people are unable to gather for a variety of reasons) and out of possibility (advances in technology access and quality). Here are a few things to consider if you decide to create a service where attendees will access it virtually.

- What is most important to the family? If they were able to hold the funeral fully in person, what would be the most important parts of it? How can you help translate those parts across space and medium?

- What can we call this event so that it describes both the event itself and reflects the personality of your loved one? Can we call the deceased to mind even more by simply giving this grief event a more personal title? Use announcements, messages, communications, posts, websites, etc., to create a very evocative entry into the event. Maintain the thread or threads throughout the event and afterwards to recreate the sense of being someplace special, and spatial, together.

- What roles do you want to create or designate? What roles do you want to have, and not want to have?

- Are the important roles, rituals, and inspirations going to be held in the place where you are, or remotely? What connections do you want to include from different places? What is needed to ensure those work correctly? Recommendation: alternate or balance internal and external roles, gestures, and rituals. Talk with people in different roles ahead of time to clarify what it looks like, especially time constraints or requests.

- Consider placing heightened attention on the arrival and departure of participants into whatever space or spaces you are using. This includes online spaces, telephone, and in-person connections. In what ways can we share a gesture or ritual to mark arrival and departure, to show our strength in numbers if not in physicality?

- Ensure participants have a way to introduce themselves. In the interest of time, it might be helpful if people write their own introduction and then they are circulated before the event. This gives people a chance to make their own personal connections during and after the event to build an even stronger community in the face of physical distance.
- Consider engaging the body in lieu of being together. Can you incorporate multiple senses? Our ability to touch each other is especially fraught right now. What can we do to incorporate texture and physicality into our rituals?
- Are there ways to send items to each participant, or for every participant to send something to the primary mourners, so there is something physical to represent their love and care? Letters sent before the service to display? Flowers? Maybe bowls or glasses of water, candles, flower stems, branches of a flowering bush, origami, or traced hands on paper with messages of love and support.

TECHNICAL QUESTIONS

- What is the general level of technical ease of the guests?
- Are there important attendees who will need extra support for setup and participation in advance?
- Is there any concern about bad actors dropping into the ceremony?
- Who can ensure that attendees have the most recent version of the technology being used?
- Online ceremonies should have a co-host who can control the features of the platform while the celebrant or participants are being present. This can also make multiple cameras possible for ceremony elements that will be shared with everyone.
- Is there a waiting room function that allows family and celebrant to prepare before attendees join? You can also move people from the event to the waiting room if they are disruptive.
- What are the most important aspects of a traditional funeral for you so that we can translate them to the online space?

- Review your customer-facing images and messages if using your own programs. For instance, Zoom allows you to personalize the waiting room image. What does yours look like now? Should it be changed?

SOUND AND VIDEO

- Will attendees use video the whole time or during specific parts?
- Will they be encouraged to use a Speaker or Gallery view?
- Will speaker videos be spotlighted/pinned?
- Will the service be recorded and do we need to announce that? Consider, when the ceremony proper begins, having everyone displayed with just their name on a black background, so that the speaker at any given moment is the only one with video and audio on.
- Does the family want screenshots of the online gallery as a memento?
- Will attendees be muted?
- Should they be allowed to mute/unmute themselves?
- How will they signify they would like to speak (i.e. raise hand in video, Participant tab, etc.)?
- Who determines who can unmute (i.e. celebrant, family, tech manager)?
- Who is allowed to share sound and visuals?

CHAT

- Would you like attendees to chat with everyone?
- Can attendees chat privately with each other?
- Will the chat be saved as an artifact for the family?
- Who will manage the chat and are they familiar with the platform you will use?

Sample Funeral for a Public Figure

Funerals of public figures are excellent opportunities to see how symbolism and ritual are woven in to personalize a service. They are also great ways to see different celebrants and religious ceremonies in action. The outline below shows the major steps for a set of ceremonies and rituals for the U.S. Representative John Lewis. Added to that, the events were held in 2020 during the Covid-19 pandemic. Altogether this was surely a very complex undertaking, in both senses of the word. The different stages of ceremonies, held in different locations, also gives you a sense of the life themes around which planners chose to organize events.

JOHN LEWIS

American politician, statesman, and civil rights activist and leader who served in the United States House of Representatives for Georgia's 5th congressional district from 1987 until his death in 2020.

Funeral ceremonies spanning from Saturday, July 25 to Thursday, July 30 and traveling from Troy, Selma, and Montgomery, Alabama, to Washington, D.C., and finally to Atlanta, Georgia.

1. The Boy From Troy - Saturday, July 25, 2020 in Troy and Selma, AL
A Service Celebrating "The Boy from Troy"
Trojan Arena, Troy University 10:00–11:00 a.m.

Rep. Lewis Lies in Repose
Trojan Arena, Troy University 11:00 a.m.–2:00 p.m.

Selma Honors Congressman John Robert Lewis: 1940-2020
Brown Chapel A.M.E. Church 6:00–8:00 p.m.

Rep. Lewis Lies in Repose
Brown Chapel A.ME. Church 8:00–11:00 p.m.

2. Good Trouble - Sunday, July 26 in Selma and Montgomery, AL
The Final Crossing, procession from Brown Chapel to the Pettus Bridge
10:00 a.m.

Receiving Ceremony
Alabama State Capitol 2:00–2:15 p.m.

Rep. John Lewis Lies in State
Alabama State Capitol 3:00–7:00 p.m.

3. The Conscience Of The Congress -Monday, July 27 and Tuesday, July 28 in Washington, D.C.
Special Ceremony
Rotunda, United States Capitol, Monday, July 27, 2:00–3:00 p.m.

Rep. John Lewis Lies in State
United States Capitol, July 27, 3:00–10:00 p.m., and July 28, 8:00 a.m.–10:00 p.m.

4. Atlanta's Servant Leader - Wednesday, July 29 in Atlanta, GA
Special Ceremony
Rotunda, Georgia State Capitol 2:00–3:00 p.m.

Rep. John Lewis Lies in State
Rotunda, Georgia State Capitol 3:00– 7:00 p.m.

Phi Beta Sigma Fraternity Omega Service
Rotunda, Georgia State Capitol 7:00– 8:00 p.m.

5. A Lifetime Of Service - Thursday, July 30 in Atlanta, GA
A Celebration of Life
Ebenezer Baptist Church Horizon Sanctuary 11:00 a.m.

6. *Interment:* **South-View Cemetery, Atlanta, GA (private)**

Public Speaking Practice

The speaking speed for funerals may be slower or have more emotional range than other ceremonies you have led. A few practice readings will help you get ready for that range and improve your enunciation. Here are four passages in a more formal style and with some tricky word combinations. Use them to practice your pacing, emphasis, enunciation, and speed. Aim for 120-150 spoken words-per-minute as a baseline. This is probably slower than you are used to. Practice getting comfortable with pauses and expressive vocalizations at specific points of your choosing. Practice speaking with a giant smile on your face for the whole speech. Practice speaking with a somber expression for the whole speech. Practice with a variety of expressions.

✦

Our father - how shall I describe our father? - was a ruined Barbados peasant, exiled in a Harlem which he loathed, where he never saw the sun or the sky he remembered, where life took place neither indoors nor without, and where there was no joy. By which I mean, no joy that he remembered. Had it been otherwise, had he been able to bring with him into the prison where he perished any of the joy he had felt on that far-off island, then the air of sea and the impulse to dance would sometimes have transformed our dreadful rooms. Our lives might have been very different. But no, he brought with him from Barbados only black rum and a blacker pride, and magic incantations which neither healed nor saved. He did not understand the people among whom he found himself, for him they had no coherence, no stature and no pride. He came from a race which had been flourishing at the very dawn of the world - a race greater and nobler than Rome or Judea, mightier than Egypt - he came from a race of kings, kings who had never been taken in battle, kings who had never been slaves. He spoke to us of tribes and empires, battles, victories and monarchs of whom we had never heard - they were not mentioned in our school books - and invested us with glories in which we felt more awkward than the secondhand shoes we wore. In the stifling room of his pretensions and expectations, we stumbled wretchedly about, stubbing our toes, as it were, on rubies, scraping our shins on golden caskets, bringing down, with a childish cry, the splendid purple tapestry on which, in pounding gold and scarlet, our destinies and inheritance were figured.

From *Tell Me How Long the Train's Been Gone* by James Baldwin [294 words]

If you are interested in stories with happy endings, you would be better off reading some other book. In this book, not only is there no happy ending, there is no happy beginning and very few happy things in the middle. This is because not very many happy things happened in the lives of the three Baudelaire youngsters. Violet, Klaus, and Sunny Baudelaire were intelligent children, and they were charming, and resourceful, and had pleasant facial features, but they were extremely unlucky, and most everything that happened to them was rife with misfortune, misery, and despair. I'm sorry to tell you this, but that is how the story goes.

Their misfortune began one day at Briny Beach. The three Baudelaire children lived with their parents in an enormous mansion at the heart of a dirty and busy city, and occasionally their parents gave them permission to take a rickety trolley-the word "rickety," you probably know, here means "unsteady" or "likely to collapse"-alone to the seashore, where they would spend the day as a sort of vacation as long as they were home for dinner. This particular morning it was gray and cloudy, which didn't bother the Baudelaire youngsters one bit. When it was hot and sunny, Briny Beach was crowded with tourists and it was impossible to find a good place to lay one's blanket. On gray and cloudy days, the Baudelaires had the beach to themselves to do what they liked.

From *The Bad Beginning* by Lemony Snicket [243 words]

All children, except one, grow up. They soon know that they will grow up, and the way Wendy knew was this. One day when she was two years old she was playing in a garden, and she plucked another flower and ran with it to her mother. I suppose she must have looked rather delightful, for Mrs. Darling put her hand to her heart and cried, "Oh, why can't you remain like this forever!" This was all that passed between them on the subject, but henceforth Wendy knew that she must grow up. You always know after you are two. Two is the beginning of the end.

Of course they lived at 14, and until Wendy came her mother was the chief one. She was a lovely lady, with a romantic mind and such a sweet mocking mouth. Her romantic mind was like the tiny boxes, one within the other, that come from the puzzling East, however many you discover there is always one more; and her sweet mocking mouth had one kiss on it that Wendy could never get, though there it was, perfectly conspicuous in the right-hand corner.

The way Mr. Darling won her was this: the many gentlemen who had been boys when she was a girl discovered simultaneously that they loved her, and they all ran to her house to propose to her except Mr. Darling, who took a cab and nipped in first, and so he got her. He got all of her, except the innermost box and the kiss. He never knew about the box, and in time he gave up trying for the kiss. Wendy thought Napoleon could have got it, but I can picture him trying, and then going off in a passion, slamming the door.

From *Peter Pan* by J.M. Barrie [295 words]

A mad boxer shot a quick, gloved jab to the jaw of his dizzy opponent. A quick movement of the enemy will jeopardize six gunboats. Fax back Jim's Gwyneth Paltrow video quiz. Perhaps President Clinton's amazing sax skills will be judged quite favorably. When we go back to Juarez, Mexico, do we fly over picturesque Arizona? My expensive quartz watch once belonged to JFK. We have just quoted on nine dozen boxes of gray lamp wicks. Six big juicy steaks sizzled in a pan as five workmen left the quarry.

Fred specialized in the job of making very quaint wax toys. William said that everything about his jacket was in quite good condition except for the zipper. Jack amazed a few girls by dropping the antique onyx vase. You can pack my box with five dozen liquor jugs. Law books forgave John Quincy Adams, sixth president. Then a cop quizzed Mick Jagger's ex-wives briefly. Jim just quit and packed extra heavy bags for Liz. You can watch all five questions asked by experts. The job of waxing linoleum frequently peeves chintzy kids. Sixty zippers were quickly picked from the woven jute bag.

From *MyFonts.com* [192 words]

Notes

For an active list of links included in the printed Notes, please see:
www.18thandfairfax.com/newamericanfunerals/notes_bibliography

INTRODUCTION

1. Inc, Gallup. 2007. "*Religion.*" Gallup.com. June 8, 2007. news. gallup.com/poll/1690/religion.aspx.
2. A. R. Blackshield, Michael Coper, David Brown, and Richard Krever. 1986. *The Judgments of Justice Lionel Murphy*. Sydney: Primavera Press.

WHY DO WE RITUALIZE OUR DEAD?

3. Alan D. Wolfelt, 2016. "Why Is the Funeral Ritual Important?" Center for Loss & Life Transition. December 16, 2016. www. centerforloss.com/2016/12/funeral-ritual-important.
4. Eric Layer. 2020. *The Right Way of Death : Restoring the American Funeral Business to Its True Calling*. Albuquerque: M Path Publishing.
5. Wolfelt, 2016. "Why Is the Funeral Ritual Important?"
6. Barry Yeoman. 2018. "When Animals Grieve." National Wildlife Federation. January 30, 2018. www.nwf.org/Home/Magazines/ National-Wildlife/2018/Feb-Mar/Animals/When-Animals-Grieve.
   (While many animals will mourn beloved others like children or partners, currently chimpanzees, magpies, and African elephants exhibit ritualized burial of their own community members, with moments of silence, preparing the body using flowers and foliage, and physical gestures.)
7. Elisabeth Kübler-Ross. 1969. *On Death and Dying*. London: Routledge.

8.   This is not meant to invalidate Kübler-Ross's fascinating and important work on death and dying, simply to counteract popular and widely held beliefs.

9.   Camille B. Wortman and Roxane C. Silver. 1989. "The Myths of Coping with Loss." *Journal of Consulting and Clinical Psychology* 57 (3): 349–57. doi.org/10.1037/0022-006x.57.3.349.

WHAT IS AN "AMERICAN FUNERAL"?

10. Research Group, Pew. 2019. "In U.S., Decline of Christianity Continues at Rapid Pace." Pew Research Center's Religion & Public Life Project. October 17, 2019. www.pewresearch.org/religion/2019/10/17/in-u-s-decline-of-christianity-continues-at-rapid-pace.

11. Gregory A. Smith. 2021. "About Three-In-Ten U.S. Adults Are Now Religiously Unaffiliated." Pew Research Center's Religion & Public Life Project. December 14, 2021. www.pewresearch.org/religion/2021/12/14/about-three-in-ten-u-s-adults-are-now-religiously-unaffiliated.

12. "New Orleans Second Line Parade | History and Traditions." n.d. NewOrleans.com. Accessed August 2, 2022. www.neworleans.com/things-to-do/music/history-and-traditions/second-lines.

13. Rachel Siegel. 2019. "Where Gun Violence Abounds, Honoring Loved Ones with 'Rest in Peace' Shirts." *Washington Post*, August 10, 2019. www.washingtonpost.com/business/2019/08/10/mass-shootings-everyday-grief-honoring-loved-ones-with-rest-peace-shirts.

14. "Roadside Memorial." 2022. Wikipedia. June 10, 2022. en.wikipedia.org/wiki/Roadside_memorial.

15. "Ghost Bike." 2021. Wikipedia. May 10, 2021. en.wikipedia.org/wiki/Ghost_bike.

16. SurferToday.com, Editor at. 2020. "Paddle-Out: The Origins of the Surfers Memorial Circle." Surfertoday. June 11, 2020. www.surfertoday.com/surfing/paddle-out-the-origins-of-the-surfers-memorial-circle.

17. "San Francisco's Chinatown Funeral Bands." 2010. YouTube. Associated Press. March 12, 2010. www.youtube.com/watch?v=gvhmCD38FrA.

18. Lee Webster. n.d. "Legal Requirements by State." New Hampshire Funeral Resources & Education. Accessed August 2, 2022. www.nhfuneral.org/legal-requirements-by-state.html.

DISPOSITION OPTIONS

19. "2021 NFDA Cremation and Burial Report." Editors. 2021. Brookfield, WI: National Funeral Directors Association.
20. "State Requirements." 2019. National Home Funeral Alliance. 2019. www.homefuneralalliance.org/state-requirements.html.
21. Ibid.
22. Editors. 2021. "2021 NFDA Cremation and Burial Report."

WHO'S WHO IN END-OF-LIFE SERVICES?

23. Maria McGinnis. 2021. "With No Clear Guidelines on Documenting Transgender Deaths, Advocates & Community Members Must Take Matters into Their Own Hands." The Buckeye Flame. September 7, 2021. www.thebuckeyeflame.com/2021/09/07/documenting-trans-deaths.

TYPES OF END-OF-LIFE CEREMONIES

24. Amy Cunningham, Funeral Director at Fitting Tribute Funeral Services (Brooklyn, NY) coined the terms *opportunities for ceremony* and *ceremony gestures* as they relate to funeral celebrants.
25. For more information visit the National Home Funeral Alliance at www.homefuneralalliance.org/state-requirements.html
26. "2021 NDFA Cremation & Burial Report," 2021. National Funeral Directors Association.

TYPICAL FUNERAL ELEMENTS AND FLOW

27. Church Of England. 1687. *The Book of Common Prayer and Administration of the Sacraments and Other Rites and Ceremonies*

of the Church of England : With the Psalter, or Psalms of David. London: Thomas Guy.

28. Christopher Klein. 2022. "Abraham Lincoln's Funeral Train: How America Mourned for Three Weeks." History. A&E Television Networks. February 7, 2022. www.history.com/news/abraham-lincoln-funeral-train.

29. "Queen Victoria's Funeral (1901)." 2014. YouTube. British Pathé. 2014. www.youtube.com/watch?v=t9yiG3EUz_A.

MAIN WRITTEN PARTS OF THE CEREMONY

30. "Humanism and Its Aspirations: Humanist Manifesto III, a Successor to the Humanist Manifesto of 1933." 2003. American Humanist Association. 2003. www.americanhumanist.org/what-is-humanism/manifesto3.

WRITING AND DELIVERING EULOGIES

31. Anne Sladon and Sara Thompson. 2008. "Funny and Wise Eulogy." YouTube. 2008. www.youtube.com/watch?v=73Qc9D3m8y8.

32. Mona Simpson. 2011. "Opinion: A Sister's Eulogy for Steve Jobs." *The New York Times*, October 30, 2011, sec. Opinion. www.nytimes.com/2011/10/30/opinion/mona-simpsons-eulogy-for-steve-jobs.html.

MUSIC

33. Bill Withers. 1971. *Ain't No Sunshine*. Vinyl. Rutherford, NJ: Sony Music Entertainment. open.spotify.com/track/1k1Bqnv2RouJXQN4u6LKYt?si=255fb6fb91a34e68.

34. Pentatonix. 2019. *The Sound of Silence*. Digital. New York, NY: RCA Records. open.spotify.com/track/0ZFeVCKCMCXUQ1TKVd2azW?si=3d090d4f7086421f.

35. Christoph Willibald Gluck. *Orfeo Ed Euridice: Dance of the Blessed Spirits (Act II)*. Performed by the Berliner

Philharmoniker. 1995. Vinyl. Hilversum, Netherlands: Deutsche Grammophon/PolyGram. open.spotify.com/ track/34gCuhDGsG4bRPIf9bbo2f?si=a9cf3bo790c44961.

36. Jule Styne. 1968. *Don't Rain on My Parade*. Performed by Barbra Streisand. Vinyl. Rutherford, NJ: Sony Music Entertainment. open.spotify.com/ track/1zf8Xmj66XRiI6Etw2Ddu7?si=c83b34eba4604d87.

RITUALS

37. Soulz Talosaga. 2015. "Tribute Hakaz for Jonah Lomu." YouTube. Rugby Rampage. 2015. www.youtube.com/ watch?v=ovd3voCPXJA.

DIFFICULT FUNERALS

38. Rosalie Kuyvenhoven. 2018. "Dementia-Friendly Funerals." Www.ritualstoday.co.uk. Rituals Today. October 22, 2018. www.ritualstoday.co.uk/how-to-have-a-dementia-friendly-funeral.

39. Robert Olson. 2018. "Suicide and Language." Centre for Suicide Prevention. Centre for Suicide Prevention. 2018. www.suicideinfo.ca/resource/suicideandlanguage.

40. Thomas Niederkrotenthaler et al. 2020. "Association between Suicide Reporting in the Media and Suicide: Systematic Review and Meta-Analysis." *BMJ*, no. 368 (March): 575. doi.org/10.1136/bmj.m575.

41. Peter S. Bearman and James Moody. 2004. "Suicide and Friendships among American Adolescents." *American Journal of Public Health* 94 (1): 89–95. doi.org/10.2105/ajph.94.1.89.

42. Robert Preit. 2016. "Family, Friends of Suicide Victims at Higher Risk." WebMD. WebMD. 2016. www.webmd.com/ mental-health/news/20160126/suicide-risk-rises-among-family-friends-of-suicide-victims-study.

43. Megan Brenan. 2018. "Americans' Strong Support for Euthanasia Persists." *Gallup*. Washington, D.C.: Gallup

Organization. news.gallup.com/poll/235145/americans-strong-support-euthanasia-persists.aspx.

44. Brandon Tensley and Veronica Stracqualursi. 2020. "Breaking down the Significance of John Lewis' Funeral Service." CNN. CNN. July 31, 2020. www.cnn.com/2020/07/31/politics/john-lewis-atlanta-funeral-service/index.html.

BUSINESS MODELS

45. "Rabbi Salary." 2022. Www.payscale.com. PayScale. July 10, 2022. www.payscale.com/research/US/Job=Rabbi/Salary.

46. Editorial Team. 2022. "How Much Do Priests Get Paid?" Indeed Career Guide. Indeed. May 3, 2022. www.indeed.com/career-advice/pay-salary/how-much-do-priests-get-paid.

47. "Gender Dominance in Funeral Service Is Changing." 2021. NFDA.org. National Funeral Directors Association. May 7, 2021. nfda.org/news/blog/gender-dominance-in-funeral-service.

48. "Arranging Funeral Director Demographics and Statistics: Number of Arranging Funeral Directors in the US." 2021. Zippia.com. Zippia. January 29, 2021. www.zippia.com/arranging-funeral-director-jobs/demographics.

49. Joan C. Williams. 2022. "Stop Asking Women of Color to Do Unpaid Diversity Work." *Washington Post*, April 14, 2022. www.washingtonpost.com/business/stop-asking-women-of-color-to-do-unpaid-diversity-work/2022/04/14/aed6f626-bc03-11ec-a92d-c763de818c21_story.html.

50. "Quantifying America's Gender Wage Gap by Race/Ethnicity." 2022. *NationalPartnership.org*. Washington, D.C.: The National Partnership for Women & Families. www.nationalpartnership.org/our-work/resources/economic-justice/fair-pay/quantifying-americas-gender-wage-gap.pdf.

51. Gus Wezerek and Kristen R. Ghodsee. 2020. "Women's Unpaid Labor Is Worth $10,900,000,000,000." *The New York Times*, March 5, 2020, sec. Opinion. www.nytimes.com/interactive/2020/03/04/opinion/women-unpaid-labor.html.

THE FUTURE OF FUNERALS

Changes in the Demographics of the Funeral Industry

52. "Arranging Funeral Director Demographics and Statistics: Number of Arranging Funeral Directors in the US." 2021. Zippia.com. Zippia. January 29, 2021. www.zippia.com/arranging-funeral-director-jobs/demographics.
53. Ibid.
54. Doug Moore. 2015. "African-American Woman Hopes to Break down Racial Barrier in Funeral Home Business." STLtoday.com. St. Louis Post Dispatch. February 15, 2015. www.stltoday.com/news/local/metro/african-american-woman-hopes-to-break-down-racial-barrier-in-funeral-home-business/article_0fdda64d-64b3-5b2e-91d4-efa3fdd051b9.html.
55. "Arranging Funeral Director Demographics and Statistics." 2021. Zippia.com.
56. Ibid.

The Intersection of Death, Environmentalism, and Real Estate

57. Matt Dayhoff. 2014. "Cemetery Overcrowding around the World – the Eye." Journal Star Photos. Journal Star. October 22, 2014. blogs.pjstar.com/eye/2014/10/22/cemetery-overcrowding-around-the-world.
58. Emiko Jozuka. 2016. "Death Is a High-Tech Trip in Japan's Futuristic Cemeteries." Vice.com. Vice. March 2, 2016. www.vice.com/en/article/9a3a5a/death-is-a-high-tech-trip-in-japans-futuristic-cemeteries.
59. Jorge Casuso. 2019. "Futuristic Architect Envisions Crematorium off Santa Monica Beach." Surfsantamonica.com. Surf Santa Monica. July 16, 2019. www.surfsantamonica.com/ssm_site/the_lookout/news/News-2019/July-2019/07_16_2017_Futuristic_Architect_Envisions_Eco_Crematorium_Off_Santa_%20Monica_Beach.html.
60. Christopher Coutts, Carlton Basmajian, Joseph Sehee, Sarah Kelty, and Patrice C. Williams. 2018. "Natural Burial as a Land

Conservation Tool in the US." *Landscape and Urban Planning* 178 (October): 130–43. doi.org/10.1016/j.landurbplan.2018.05.022.

Personalization and Decolonizing the Death Experience

61. Richard Fry and Kim Parker. 2018. "Early Benchmarks Show 'Post-Millennials' on Track to Be Most Diverse, Best-Educated Generation Yet." Pew Research Center. Social & Demographic Trends Project. Pew Research Center. November 15, 2018. www.pewsocialtrends.org/2018/11/15/early-benchmarks-show-post-millennials-on-track-to-be-most-diverse-best-educated-generation-yet.

62. Katya Moorman. 2019. "Die Fabulously: Rethinking What We Wear in the Casket." NoKillMag. No Kill Magazine. June 17, 2019. www.nokillmag.com/articles/die-fabulously.

63. Kami Fletcher. 2019. "Decolonizing Death Studies." Radical Death Studies. The Collective for Radical Death Studies. August 10, 2019. radicaldeathstudies.com/2019/08/10/decolonizing-death-studies.

64. Brad Rex. 2015. A Good Goodbye: Reinventing the Funeral Experience. Interview by Gail Rubin. *Funeral Radio.* funeralradio.com/a-good-goodbye/reinventing-the-funeral-experience-with-brad-rex.

65. Phineas Harper. 2016. "'My Trainers Are More Customised than My Funeral.'" Dezeen.com. Dezeen. November 24, 2016. www.dezeen.com/2016/11/24/death-design-trainers-more-customised-than-funeral-rituals-phineas-harper-opinion.

Technology

66. Cremation Association of North America. 2020. "Industry Professionals Discuss the Future of Funerals." Webinar. ConnectingDirectors.com. Connecting Directors. November 17, 2020. connectingdirectors.com/58048-industry-professionals-discuss-the-future-of-funerals.

67. Chris Godfrey. 2019. "The Griefbot That Could Change How We Mourn." *The Daily Beast,* April 29, 2019, sec. science. www.

thedailybeast.com/the-griefbot-that-could-change-how-we-mourn.

68. Alex Martin. 2017. "High Tech, IT and Robots Are at Forefront of Japan's Funeral Industry Boom." JapanTimes.com. The Japan Times. September 25, 2017. www.japantimes.co.jp/news/2017/09/25/reference/high-tech-robots-forefront-japans-funeral-industry-boom.

69. Lex Berko. 2014. "Death on the Internet: The Rise of Livestreaming Funerals." TheAtlantic.com. The Atlantic. December 15, 2014. www.theatlantic.com/technology/archive/2014/12/death-on-the-internet-the-rise-of-livestreaming-funerals/383646.

70. Amy Frearson. 2020. "Common Accounts Designs an Eco-Friendly Funeral for the Digital Age." Dezeen.com. Dezeen. February 29, 2020. www.dezeen.com/2020/02/29/common-accounts-eco-friendly-funeral-virtual-afterlife.

Economic Factors

71. Eleanor Cummins. 2021. "How 'Big Funeral' Made the Afterlife so Expensive." Wired. Conde Nast. October 1, 2021. www.wired.com/story/death-funeral-industry-lobbying-politics-health.

72. William G. Gale, Hilary Gelfond, Jason Fichtner, and Benjamin H. Harris. 2020. "The Wealth of Generations, with Special Attention to the Millennials." *Brookings.com*. Brookings. www.brookings.edu/wp-content/uploads/2020/05/Generations-Working-Paper-2.pdf.

Design and Aesthetics

73. Several examples show a range of new approaches to end-of-life arrangements, design, and rituals. Consider London's newest modern funeral home, Professor Neri Oxman's death masks, and even the variety of funeral urns now available:

"Exit Here." 2022. Exit Here. 2022. www.exithere.com.

"Neri Oxman's New Death Masks Contain Pigment-Producing Microorganisms." 2018. Video. YouTube. Dezeen. April 26, 2018. www.youtube.com/watch?v=9gow6rpjvvE.

Elizabeth Stokes. n.d. "Urns and Funeral Vessels." Pinterest. www.pinterest.com/ceremoniesforlifeanddeath/urns-and-other-vessels.

The Customer Experience and Everything Under One Roof

74. Some of the many companies and organizations offering improved customer experiences for end-of-life needs are:

    Funeral Consumers Alliance, funerals.org

    Cake. www.joincake.com

    Funeral Wise. www.funeralwise.com

    Inmemori. en.inmemori.com

    Lantern. www.lantern.co

    RoundGlass EOL. roundglass.com/living/end-of-life

Generational Impact

75. Editors. 2017. "U.S. Population by Generation, 2017." Statista. com. Statista. 2017. www.statista.com/statistics/797321/us-population-by-generation.
76. Eleanor Cummins. 2020. "Why Millennials Are the 'Death Positive' Generation." Vox. VoxMedia. January 15, 2020. www.vox.com/the-highlight/2020/1/15/21059189/death-millennials-funeral-planning-cremation-green-positive.

Bibliography

For an active list of links included in the printed Bibliography, please see: www.18thandfairfax.com/newamericanfunerals/notes_bibliography

Amanik, Allan, and Kami Fletcher. 2020. *Till Death Do Us Part: American Ethnic Cemeteries as Borders Uncrossed.* Jackson, MS: University Press Of Mississippi.

Archer, Nicole. 2020. "Funerals Are Expensive, Broken and Exploitative. They Have to Change." CNET. CNET. May 25, 2020. www.cnet.com/culture/features/funerals-are-expensive-broken-exploitative-they-have-to-change.

"Arranging Funeral Director Demographics and Statistics: Number of Arranging Funeral Directors in the US." 2021. Zippia.com. Zippia. January 29, 2021. www.zippia.com/arranging-funeral-director-jobs/demographics.

Baldwin, James. 2018. *Tell Me How Long the Train's Been Gone.* United Kingdom: Penguin Books.

Baron, Michelle Renee. 2011. "Queering US Public Mourning Rituals: Funerals, Performance, and the Construction of Normativity." Dissertation, University of California, Berkeley. escholarship.org/content/qt0qc7655c/qt0qc7655c_noSplash_0340f664e859e893279491ea9797238c.pdf.

Barrie, J M, and David Wyatt. 2007. *Peter Pan.* Oxford: Oxford University Press.

Bearman, Peter S., and James Moody. 2004. "Suicide and Friendships among American Adolescents." *American Journal of Public Health* 94 (1): 89–95. doi.org/10.2105/ajph.94.1.89.

Beck, Renee, and Sydney Barbara Metrick. 1990. *The Art of Ritual : A Guide to Creating and Performing Your Own Rituals for Growth and Change*. Berkeley, Calif.: Celestial Arts.

Belk, Donna, and Kateyanne Unullisi. 2015. *Las Ceremonias Bonitas : Ceremonies for Home Funerals*. United States: Sugar Skull Publishing.

Bell, Catherine. 2009. *Ritual : Perspectives and Dimensions*. New York: Oxford University Press.

Berko, Lex. 2014. "Death on the Internet: The Rise of Livestreaming Funerals." TheAtlantic.com. The Atlantic. December 15, 2014. www.theatlantic.com/technology/archive/2014/12/death-on-the-internet-the-rise-of-livestreaming-funerals/383646.

Brenan, Megan. 2018. "Americans' Strong Support for Euthanasia Persists." *Gallup*. Washington, D.C.: Gallup Organization. news.gallup.com/poll/235145/americans-strong-support-euthanasia-persists.aspx.

Browne, Ray B. 1980. *Rituals and Ceremonies in Popular Culture*. Bowling Green, Ohio: Bowling Green University Popular Press.

Burch, Kevin. 2013. *Eulogy Made Simple: How to Write and Deliver a Great Funeral Speech in Six Simple Steps*. Empowering Publications.

Butler, Katy. 2019. *The Art of Dying Well : A Practical Guide to a Good End of Life*. New York: Scribner, An Imprint Of Simon & Schuster, Inc.

Carson, Denise. 2011. *Parting Ways : New Rituals and Celebrations of Life's Passing*. Berkeley, Calif.: University Of California Press.

Casuso, Jorge. 2019. "Futuristic Architect Envisions Crematorium off Santa Monica Beach." SurfSantaMonica.com. Surf Santa Monica. July 16, 2019. www.surfsantamonica.com/ssm_site/the_lookout/news/News-2019/July-2019/07_16_2017_

Futuristic_Architect_Envisions_Eco_Crematorium_Off_
Santa_%20Monica_Beach.html.

CDFuneralNews. 2020. "Industry Professionals Discuss the Future
of Funerals." ConnectingDirectors.com. Connecting
Directors. November 17, 2020. www.connectingdirectors.
com/58048-industry-professionals-discuss-the-future-of-
funerals.

Chavez, Sarah. 2020. "Trans Death Rights Are Human Rights." The
Order of the Good Death. The Order of the Good Death.
March 14, 2020. www.orderofthegooddeath.com/article/
trans-death-rights-are-human-rights.

Church Of England. 1687. *The Book of Common Prayer and
Administration of the Sacraments and Other Rites and
Ceremonies of the Church of England : With the Psalter, or Psalms
of David.* London: Thomas Guy.

Connell, Elton. 2022. "Trans Living Wills." F Newsmagazine. March
31, 2022. fnewsmagazine.com/2022/03/trans-living-wills.

Coogler, Ryan, dir. 2018. *Black Panther*. Film. Burbank, CA: Marvel
Studios.

Coutts, Christopher, Carlton Basmajian, Joseph Sehee, Sarah
Kelty, and Patrice C. Williams. 2018. "Natural Burial
as a Land Conservation Tool in the US." *Landscape and
Urban Planning* 178 (October): 130–43. doi.org/10.1016/j.
landurbplan.2018.05.022.

Cummins, Eleanor. 2020. "Why Millennials Are the 'Death Positive'
Generation." Vox. VoxMedia. January 15, 2020. www.vox.com/
the-highlight/2020/1/15/21059189/death-millennials-funeral-
planning-cremation-green-positive.

Cummins, Eleanor. 2021. "How 'Big Funeral' Made the Afterlife so
Expensive." Wired. Conde Nast. October 1, 2021. www.wired.
com/story/death-funeral-industry-lobbying-politics-health.

Dayhoff, Matt. 2014. "Cemetery Overcrowding around the World – the Eye." Journal Star Photos. Journal Star. October 22, 2014. blogs.pjstar.com/eye/2014/10/22/cemetery-overcrowding-around-the-world.

Dillman, Erika. 2011. *The Party of Your Life : How to Plan a Funeral That Reflects Your Interests, Achievements and Taste.* Santa Monica, Calif.: Santa Monica ; London.

Doughty, Caitlin, and Landis Blair. 2019. *From Here to Eternity: Traveling the World to Find the Good Death.* London: Weidenfeld & Nicolson.

Doughty, Caitlin, and Dr. Kami Fletcher. 2020. "Why Are Black & White Funeral Homes STILL Separate?" YouTube.com. Ask A Mortician. 18, 2020. www.youtube.com/watch?v=W4-oiAz FIcI&list=PLSaSadX18ksoX1UHAo_o7F2R3pMFiPoNT&in dex=4.

Easton, Steacy. 2018. "Trans-Death: Exploring Deadnaming through a Death Positive Lens." TalkDeath. Talk Death. July 2, 2018. www.talkdeath.com/trans-death-exploring-deadnaming-death-positive-lens.

Ed. 2017. "U.S. Population by Generation, 2017." Statista.com. Statista. 2017. www.statista.com/statistics/797321/us-population-by-generation.

Editorial Team. 2022. "How Much Do Priests Get Paid?" Indeed Career Guide. Indeed. May 3, 2022. www.indeed.com/career-advice/pay-salary/how-much-do-priests-get-paid.

Editors. 2021. "2021 NFDA Cremation and Burial Report." Brookfield, WI: National Funeral Directors Association.

Egan, Kerry. 2016. *On Living.* New York: Riverhead Books.

"Exit Here." 2022. Exit Here. 2022. www.exithere.com.

"FAMIC Study." 2015. Famic.org. Funeral and Memorial Information Council. 2015. www.famic.org/famic-study.

Fletcher, Kami. 2018. "Race & the Funeral Profession: What Jessica Mitford Missed." TalkDeath.com. Talk Death. December 2, 2018. www.talkdeath.com/race-funeral-profession-what-jessica-mitford-missed.

Fletcher, Kami. 2019. "Decolonizing Death Studies." Radical Death Studies. The Collective for Radical Death Studies. August 10, 2019. www.radicaldeathstudies.com/2019/08/10/decolonizing-death-studies.

Frearson, Amy. 2020. "Common Accounts Designs an Eco-Friendly Funeral for the Digital Age." Dezeen.com. Dezeen. February 29, 2020. www.dezeen.com/2020/02/29/common-accounts-eco-friendly-funeral-virtual-afterlife.

Fry, Richard, and Kim Parker. 2018. "Early Benchmarks Show 'Post-Millennials' on Track to Be Most Diverse, Best-Educated Generation Yet." Pew Research Center. Social & Demographic Trends Project. Pew Research Center. November 15, 2018. www.pewsocialtrends.org/2018/11/15/early-benchmarks-show-post-millennials-on-track-to-be-most-diverse-best-educated-generation-yet.

Gale, William G., Hilary Gelfond, Jason Fichtner, and Benjamin H. Harris. 2020. "The Wealth of Generations, with Special Attention to the Millennials." *Brookings.com*. Brookings. www.brookings.edu/wp-content/uploads/2020/05/Generations-Working-Paper-2.pdf.

Ganger, Brigitte. 2121. "Gender in Obits: Addressing Trans, Non-Binary and Identity Issues in Obituaries." BeyondTheDash.com. June 11, 2121. www.beyondthedash.com/blog/obituary-writing/gender-in-obits-addressing-trans-non-binary/7338.

Gayden Metcalfe, and Charlotte Hays. 2015. *Being Dead Is No Excuse : The Official Southern Ladies Guide to Hosting the Perfect Funeral*. New York: Hachette Books.

"Gender Dominance in Funeral Service Is Changing." 2021. NFDA.org. National Funeral Directors Association. May 7, 2021.

www.nfda.org/news/blog/gender-dominance-in-funeral-service.

"Ghost Bike." 2021. Wikipedia. May 10, 2021. en.wikipedia.org/wiki/Ghost_bike.

Gluck, Christoph Willibald, and Berliner Philharmoniker. 1995. *Orfeo Ed Euridice: Dance of the Blessed Spirits (Act II)*. Vinyl. Hilversum, Netherlands: Deutsche Grammophon/PolyGram. open.spotify.com/track/34gCuhDGsG4bRPIf9bbo2f?si=a9cf3bo790c44961.

Godfrey, Chris. 2019. "The Griefbot That Could Change How We Mourn." *The Daily Beast*, April 29, 2019, sec. science. www.thedailybeast.com/the-griefbot-that-could-change-how-we-mourn.

Grimes, Ronald L. 2014. *The Craft of Ritual Studies*. Oxford: Oxford University Press.

Halifax, Joan. 2014. *Being with Dying : Cultivating Compassion and Fearlessness in the Presence of Death*. Boston: Shambhala.

Harper, Phineas. 2016. "'My Trainers Are More Customised than My Funeral.'" Dezeen.com. Dezeen. November 24, 2016. www.dezeen.com/2016/11/24/death-design-trainers-more-customised-than-funeral-rituals-phineas-harper-opinion.

Hayhurst, Ash. 2019. "Making Informed Choices Wehen Planning a Funeral: A Guide for Queer People." *The Good Grief Trust*. London, England: The Good Grief Trust. www.thegoodgrieftrust.org/wp-content/uploads/2019/07/Standard-PDF-queer-funeral-guide.pdf.

Hebb, Michael. 2019. *Let's Talk about Death (over Dinner)*. London: Orion Books.

Herring, Lucinda. 2019. *Reimagining Death : Stories and Practical Wisdom for Home Funerals and Green Burials*. Berkeley: North Atlantic Books.

Hill, Jeff, and Peggy Daniels Becker. 2008. *Life Events and Rites of Passage : The Customs and Symbols of Major Life-Cycle Milestones, Including Cultural, Secular, and Religious Traditions Observed in the United States.* Detroit, Mi: Omnigraphics.

Hills, Han. 2015. *The Humanist and Non-Religious Celebrant Handbook.*

"Home Funeral Laws." n.d. Nolo.com. Nolo Press. Accessed August 2, 2022. www.nolo.com/legal-encyclopedia/home-funeral-laws.

Homer, A T Murray, and William F Wyatt. 2003. *Iliad.* Cambridge, Mass.: Harvard University Press.

Hoy, William G. 2013. *Do Funerals Matter? The Purposes and Practices of Death Rituals in Global Perspective.* New York, NY: Routledge.

"Humanism and Its Aspirations: Humanist Manifesto III, a Successor to the Humanist Manifesto of 1933." 2003. American Humanist Association. 2003. www.americanhumanist.org/what-is-humanism/manifesto3.

Iserson, Kenneth V. 2001. *Death to Dust : What Happens to Dead Bodies?* Tucson, Az: Galen Press.

Jane Wynne Willson. 1989. *Funerals without God.* British Humanist Association.

Jean-Paul Sartre. 1946. *Existentialism Is a Humanism : (L'Existentialisme Est Un Humanisme).* New Haven: Yale University Press.

Jeltje Gordon-Lennox. 2017. *Crafting Secular Ritual : A Practical Guide.* London; Philadelphia: Jessica Kingsley Publishers.

Jozuka, Emiko. 2016. "Death Is a High-Tech Trip in Japan's Futuristic Cemeteries." Vice.com. Vice. March 2, 2016. www.vice.com/en/article/9a3a5a/death-is-a-high-tech-trip-in-japans-futuristic-cemeteries.

Klein, Christopher. 2022. "Abraham Lincoln's Funeral Train: How America Mourned for Three Weeks." History. A&E Television Networks. February 7, 2022. www.history.com/news/abraham-lincoln-funeral-train.

Kübler-Ross, Elisabeth. 1969. *On Death and Dying*. London: Routledge.

Kuyvenhoven, Rosalie. 2018. "Dementia-Friendly Funerals." RitualsToday.co.uk. Rituals Today. October 22, 2018. www.ritualstoday.co.uk/how-to-have-a-dementia-friendly-funeral.

Lamont, Corliss, Beth K. Lamont, and J. Sierra Oliva. 2011. *A Humanist Funeral Service and Celebration*. Amherst, NY: Prometheus Books.

Layer, Eric. 2020. *The Right Way of Death : Restoring the American Funeral Business to Its True Calling*. Albuquerque: M Path Publishing.

"Legal Encyclopedia, Legal Forms, Law Books, & Software." 2022. Nolo.com. 2022. www.nolo.com.

London, Eileen, and Belinda Recio. 2005. *Sacred Rituals : Connecting with Spirit through Labyrinths, Sand Paintings & Other Traditional Arts*. Gloucester, Mass.: Fair Winds ; Hove.

Loss, Center for. 2016. "Why Is the Funeral Ritual Important?" Center for Loss & Life Transition. December 16, 2016. www.centerforloss.com/2016/12/funeral-ritual-important.

Lynch, Thomas. 2009. *The Undertaking : Life Studies from the Dismal Trade*. New York: W.W. Norton.

M Casey Jarman, and Brooke Weeber. 2016. *Death : An Oral History*. San Francisco, Ca: Pulp.

Magnusson, Margareta. 2019. *Gentle Art of Swedish Death Cleaning*. Canongate Books.

Martin, Alex. 2017. "High Tech, IT and Robots Are at Forefront of Japan's Funeral Industry Boom." JapanTimes.com. The Japan Times. September 25, 2017. www.japantimes.co.jp/news/2017/09/25/reference/high-tech-robots-forefront-japans-funeral-industry-boom.

McGinnis, Maria. 2021. "With No Clear Guidelines on Documenting Transgender Deaths, Advocates & Community Members Must Take Matters into Their Own Hands." The Buckeye Flame. September 7, 2021. www.thebuckeyeflame.com/2021/09/07/documenting-trans-deaths.

Meyer, Elizabeth. 2016. *Good Mourning*. Gallery Books.

Mitford, Jessica. 2013. *The American Way of Death Revisited*. New York Vintage Books New York Vintage Books.

Moore, Doug. 2015. "African-American Woman Hopes to Break down Racial Barrier in Funeral Home Business." STLtoday.com. St. Louis Post Dispatch. February 15, 2015. www.stltoday.com/news/local/metro/african-american-woman-hopes-to-break-down-racial-barrier-in-funeral-home-business/article_0fdda64d-64b3-5b2e-91d4-efa3fdd051b9.html.

Moore, Faith. 2009. *Celebrating a Life : Planning Memorial Services and Other Creative Remembrances*. New York: Stewart, Tabori & Chang.

Moorman, Katya. 2019. "Die Fabulously: Rethinking What We Wear in the Casket." NoKillMag. No Kill Magazine. June 17, 2019. www.nokillmag.com/articles/die-fabulously.

Murphy, Lionel, A R Blackshield, Michael Coper, David Brown, and Richard Krever. 1986. *The Judgments of Justice Lionel Murphy*. Sydney: Primavera Press.

Native Land Digital. Interactive Tool. 2019. "Whose Land Are You On?" Native-Land. 2019. www.native-land.ca.

"New Orleans Second Line Parade" n.d. NewOrleans.com. Accessed August 2, 2022. www.neworleans.com/things-to-do/music/history-and-traditions/second-lines.

"NFDA General Price List Study Shows Funeral Costs Not Rising as Fast as Rate of Inflation." 2021. Nfda.org. National Funeral Directors Association. 2021. nfda.org/news/media-center/nfda-news-releases/id/6182/2021-nfda-general-price-list-study-shows-funeral-costs-not-rising-as-fast-as-rate-of-inflation.

Niederkrotenthaler, Thomas, Marlies Braun, Jane Pirkis, Benedikt Till, Steven Stack, Mark Sinyor, Ulrich S Tran, et al. 2020. "Association between Suicide Reporting in the Media and Suicide: Systematic Review and Meta-Analysis." *BMJ*, no. 368 (March): 575. doi.org/10.1136/bmj.m575.

Olson, Robert. 2018. "Suicide and Language." Centre for Suicide Prevention. Centre for Suicide Prevention. 2018. www.suicideinfo.ca/resource/suicideandlanguage.

Oxman, Neri. 2018. "Neri Oxman's New Death Masks Contain Pigment-Producing Microorganisms." Video. *Dezeen, YouTube.* www.youtube.com/watch?v=9gow6rpjvvE.

Pema Chödrön. 2017. *When Things Fall Apart : Heart Advice for Difficult Times.* London Thorsons Classics.

Pentatonix. 2019. *The Sound of Silence.* Digital. New York, NY: RCA Records. open.spotify.com/track/oZFeVCKCMCXUQ1TKV-d2azW?si=3d09od4f7086421f.

PhD, Stephen G. Hall. 2020. "Black Grief and Mourning in a Pandemic and Uprising." GoodMenProject.com. The Good Men Project. August 9, 2020. www.goodmenproject.com/featured-content/black-grief-and-mourning-in-a-pandemic-and-uprising-kami-fletcher.

Piel, Alexander K., and Fiona A. Stewart. 2015. *Death Rituals, Social Order and the Archaeology of Immortality in the Ancient*

World. Edited by Colin Renfrew, Michael J. Boyd, and Iain Morley. Cambridge University Press. doi.org/10.1017/cbo9781316014509.

Preit, Robert. 2016. "Family, Friends of Suicide Victims at Higher Risk." WebMD. WebMD. 2016. www.webmd.com/mental-health/news/20160126/suicide-risk-rises-among-family-friends-of-suicide-victims-study.

"Quantifying America's Gender Wage Gap by Race/Ethnicity." 2022. *NationalPartnership.org*. Washington, D.C.: The National Partnership for Women & Families. www.nationalpartnership.org/our-work/resources/economic-justice/fair-pay/quantifying-americas-gender-wage-gap.pdf.

"Queen Victoria's Funeral (1901)." 2014. Www.youtube.com. British Pathé. 2014. www.youtube.com/watch?v=t9yiG3EUz_A.

"Rabbi Salary." 2022. Www.payscale.com. PayScale. July 10, 2022. www.payscale.com/research/US/Job=Rabbi/Salary.

Reid, Dayna. 2015. *Funerals & Memorials : Creating the Perfect Service to Remember a Loved One*. Createspace Independent Publishing.

"Representative John Lewis Funeral Service in Atlanta, Georgia." 2020. Television. C-SPAN. www.c-span.org/video/?474223-1/representative-john-lewis-funeral-service-atlanta-georgia.

Research Group, Pew. 2019. "In U.S., Decline of Christianity Continues at Rapid Pace." Pew Research Center's Religion & Public Life Project. October 17, 2019. www.pewresearch.org/religion/2019/10/17/in-u-s-decline-of-christianity-continues-at-rapid-pace.

Rex, Brad. 2015. A Good Goodbye: Reinventing the Funeral Experience. Interview by Gail Rubin. *Funeral Radio*. funeralradio.com/a-good-goodbye/reinventing-the-funeral-experience-with-brad-rex.

"Roadside Memorial." 2022. Wikipedia. June 10, 2022. https://
en.wikipedia.org/wiki/Roadside_memorial.

"San Francisco's Chinatown Funeral Bands." 2010. Www.youtube.
com. Associated Press. March 12, 2010. www.youtube.com/
watch?v=gvhmCD38FrA.

Searl, Edward. 2000. *In Memoriam : A Guide to Modern Funeral and
Memorial Services*. Boston, Ma: Skinner House Books.

Siegel, Rachel. 2019. "Where Gun Violence Abounds, Honoring
Loved Ones with 'Rest in Peace' Shirts." *Washington
Post*, August 10, 2019. www.washingtonpost.com/
business/2019/08/10/mass-shootings-everyday-grief-honoring-
loved-ones-with-rest-peace-shirts.

Simpson, Mona. 2011. "A Sister's Eulogy for Steve Jobs." *The New
York Times*, October 30, 2011, sec. Opinion. www.nytimes.
com/2011/10/30/opinion/mona-simpsons-eulogy-for-steve-
jobs.html.

Singleton, Amanda. 2019. "Prepare a Digital Estate Plan." AARP.
com. AARP. June 11, 2019. www.aarp.org/caregiving/
financial-legal/info-2019/digital-assets-planning.html.

Sladon, Anne, and Sara Thompson. 2008. "Funny and Wise
Eulogy." Www.youtube.com. 2008. www.youtube.com/
watch?v=73Qc9D3m8y8.

Smith, Gregory A. 2021. "About Three-In-Ten U.S. Adults Are Now
Religiously Unaffiliated." Pew Research Center's Religion &
Public Life Project. December 14, 2021. www.pewresearch.
org/religion/2021/12/14/about-three-in-ten-u-s-adults-are-
now-religiously-unaffiliated.

Snicket, Lemony. 2007. *The Bad Beginning*. Bt Bound.

"State Requirements." 2019. National Home Funeral Alliance. 2019.
www.homefuneralalliance.org/state-requirements.html.

Stokes, Elizabeth. n.d. "Urns and Funeral Vessels." Pinterest. www.pinterest.com/ceremoniesforlifeanddeath/urns-and-other-vessels.

Styne, Jule, and Barbra Streisand. 1968. *Don't Rain on My Parade*. Vinyl. Rutherford, NJ: Sony Music Entertainment. open.spotify.com/track/1zf8Xmj66XRiI6Etw2Ddu7?si=c83b34eba4604d87.

SurferToday.com, Editor at. 2020. "Paddle-Out: The Origins of the Surfers Memorial Circle." Surfertoday. June 11, 2020. www.surfertoday.com/surfing/paddle-out-the-origins-of-the-surfers-memorial-circle.

Swanson, Jon. 2020. *Giving a Life Meaning: How to Lead Funerals, Memorial Services & Celebrations of Life*. Fort Wayne, IN: Emerald Hope Publishing.

Talosaga, Soulz. 2015. "Tribute Hakaz for Jonah Lomu." Www.youtube.com. Rugby Rampage. 2015. www.youtube.com/watch?v=0vd3v0CPXJA.

Taylor, Vanessa. 2022. "Inside the Rise of Human Composting and Other Green Burial Practices." Mic.com. BDG Media. April 21, 2022. www.mic.com/impact/green-funerals-burials-human-composting.

Tensley, Brandon, and Veronica Stracqualursi. 2020. "Breaking down the Significance of John Lewis' Funeral Service." CNN. CNN. July 31, 2020. www.cnn.com/2020/07/31/politics/john-lewis-atlanta-funeral-service/index.html.

Tonkin, Lois. 1996. "Growing around Grief—Another Way of Looking at Grief and Recovery." *Bereavement Care* 15 (1): 10–10. doi.org/10.1080/02682629608657376.

Turner, Christine, dir. 2013. *Homegoings*. Film. New York, NY: Maysles Cinema.

"Understanding Privilege and Oppression." 2018. *Vanderbilt.edu*. www.vanderbilt.edu/oacs/wp-content/uploads/sites/140/ Understanding-Privilege-and-Oppression-Handout.doc.

Webster, Lee. 2019. "Green Burial Council." Green Burial Council. 2019. www.greenburialcouncil.org.

Webster, Lee. n.d. "Legal Requirements by State." New Hampshire Funeral Resources & Education. Accessed August 2, 2022. www.nhfuneral.org/legal-requirements-by-state.html.

Westendorp, Mariske, and Hannah Gould. 2021. "Re-Feminizing Death: Gender, Spirituality and Death Care in the Anthropocene." *Religions* 12 (8): 667. doi.org/10.3390/ rel12080667.

Wezerek, Gus, and Kristen R. Ghodsee. 2020. "Women's Unpaid Labor Is Worth $10,900,000,000,000." *The New York Times*, March 5, 2020, sec. Opinion. www.nytimes.com/ interactive/2020/03/04/opinion/women-unpaid-labor.html.

Williams, Joan C. 2022. "Stop Asking Women of Color to Do Unpaid Diversity Work." *Washington Post*, April 14, 2022. www.washingtonpost.com/business/stop-asking-women- of-color-to-do-unpaid-diversity-work/2022/04/14/aed6f626- bc03-11ec-a92d-c763de818c21_story.html.

Withers, Bill. 1971. *Ain't No Sunshine*. Vinyl. Rutherford, NJ: Sony Music Entertainment. open.spotify.com/ track/1k1Bqnv2RouJXQN4u6LKYt?si=255fb6fb91a34e68.

Wolfelt, Alan. 2003. *Creating Meaningful Funeral Experiences : A Guide for Caregivers*. Fort Collins, Co: Companion Press.

Wolfelt, Alan. 2004. *Funeral Home Customer Service a to Z : Creating Exceptional Experiences for Today's Families*. Fort Collins, Colo.: Companion Press.

Wortman, Camille B., and Roxane C. Silver. 1989. "The Myths of Coping with Loss." *Journal of Consulting and Clinical Psychology* 57 (3): 349–57. doi.org/10.1037/0022-006x.57.3.349.

Yeoman, Barry. 2018. "When Animals Grieve." National Wildlife Federation. January 30, 2018. www.nwf.org/Home/ Magazines/National-Wildlife/2018/Feb-Mar/Animals/When-Animals-Grieve.

Yin, Karen. 2022. "Conscious Language + Design." ConsciousStyleGuide.com. Quiet Press. 2022. www.consciousstyleguide.com.

York, Sarah. 2000. *Remembering Well : Rituals for Celebrating Life and Mourning Death*. San Francisco, Calif.: Jossey-Bass.

Author Biography

Elizabeth Nordberg Stokes is a Humanist celebrant supporting atheists, agnostics, the unchurched, and the spiritual-not-religious of the greater Boston area. She has been an active funeral celebrant for five years and teaches *End-of-Life Ceremonies and Celebrations* at Celebrant Academy.

Prior to her work as a celebrant, Elizabeth was a developmental editor focusing on fiction and memoir. She lives in Cambridge, Massachusetts.

www.ingramcontent.com/pod-product-compliance
Lightning Source LLC
Chambersburg PA
CBHW020233130626
46549CB00005B/1873